1983

# Motivating Kids
## Through
# Play

# DEDICATION

Dedicated to our parents, whose love and joy in life helped us believe in ourselves and strive to find success and happiness.

- Linda K. Bunker
  Candine E. Johnson
  Jane E. Parker

# Motivating Kids Through Play

*Linda K. Bunker*
*Candine E. Johnson*
*Jane E. Parker*

*University of Virginia*
*Charlottesville, Virginia*

Leisure Press
P.O. Box 3
West Point, NY 10996

A publication of Leisure Press.
P.O. Box 3, West Point, N.Y. 10996
Copyright © 1982 Leisure Press
All rights reserved. Printed in the U.S.A.

Library of Congress Catalog Card No. 81-85625
ISBN 0-918438-22-5

Front cover photo: Janeart Inc.

The activity which is the subject of this report was produced under a grant from the U.S. Department of Education, under the auspices of the Women's Educational Equity Act. However, the opinions expressed herein do not necessarily reflect the position or policy of the Department of Education and no official endorsement should be inferred.

# CONTENTS

# ACKNOWLEDGEMENTS

The material and ideas in this manual are the result of our interactions with many individuals. In particular we are indebted to the members of Project RAMP (Raising Achievement Motivation Through Play): David Cook, Mike McPherson, Jeannie Meisky, Sarah Odom, and Pam Walker. In addition, several professional colleagues provided ideas, encouragement and insights. Our interactions with MiMi Murray, DeDe Owens, Robert Rotella and Diane Wakat are indeed valued and appreciated.

Editorial and organization support was provided by many individuals. Specific assistance from Josué Cruz, Joan Franks, and Sherry Kraft is gratefully acknowledged. A deeply sincere thank you is also extended to Karen Payne and Nina Seaman for their secretarial skills and support services. Without the help and guidance of these individuals this project would not have been possible.

The support of the University of Virginia, the Women's Educational Equity Act Program, and the U.S. Department of Education was greatly appreciated as we persevered in completing this task. Their belief in the value of this project provided great motivation.

Special photographic assistance was provided by Marlis Mann, Stanford University and University of Virginia.

# PREFACE

## HOW TO USE THIS MATERIAL

*Motivating Kids Through Play* is designed to help parents understand their children and the importance of play. There are many activity ideas and self-testing questionnaires. These are designed to aid you in becoming actively involved in the life of your child.

Read each chapter of the book. It is designed to be an action oriented approach to helping your child. The activities provided should also be tried. Answer the questions about your own feelings and those of your child. Try the many activity ideas and then feel free to create your own activities.

**L.K.B.**
**C.E.J.**
**J.E.P.**

# 1
# YOU AND YOUR CHILD

Key issues to be addressed in this chapter:
- Playing is Important
- Providing for Exploration Teaches Independence and Self Worth
- Providing Positive Reinforcement Develops Positive Attitudes
- Learning to "Do Your Best" is Important
- Serving as a Role Model

## PLAYING IS IMPORTANT

Helping children grow to their ultimate potential is an important task for all adults. Motivating children to "become the best that they can be" is an essential component of that task.

Play is of tremendous value in your child's life. Through play, your child develops his or her physical, cognitive, and social-emotional skills. Each child learns and grows through play. This learning includes specific information about self, as well as information about adults, other individuals, and the world at large.

Your child's world, a world centered on play, provides the base for everything which is to be learned. You must help your child as you provide a positive, supporting and challenging life for your child.

Remember:
   Children who live with criticism, learn to condemn.
   Children who live with hostility, learn to fight.
   Children who live with fear, learn to be apprehensive.
   Children who live with encouragement, learn to be confident.
   Children who live with praise, learn to be appreciative.
   Children who live with approval, learn to like themselves.
   Children who live with recognition, learn to have a goal.
   Children who live with honesty, learn the value of trust.

                                   —Author Unknown

As a parent, you must supply the support and environment for your child's development. The lessons of life are learned early in childhood. Your support, understanding, and the freedom you give are very important. You must understand your child and his or her unique developmental needs.

You are a very important person in the life of your child. Guiding children to help them reach their fullest potential requires intelligence and kindness. It can be made easier by taking the information presented, and following the suggestions with warmth and concern. Children must be helped to feel good about themselves and to accept responsibility for finding solutions to their own problems.

Play is the most natural form of behavior for your child. Motivating children through play is therefore a natural way to influence your child. Play is your child's world. Playing is important because it provides the information to learn about self and others.

# PROVIDING FOR EXPLORATION TEACHES INDEPENDENCE AND SELF-WORTH

You have the chance to create a situation or take advantage of natural situations that invite your child to discover and explore new ways to achieve tasks, such as *all* the different ways a single piece of playground equipment can be used. Children can be encouraged to explore further by being allowed to discover the solution to a task. With your *selective* input in the form of questions, your child can be encouraged to strive even more. Children thrive on discovery. When provided with the opportunity to discover through play, the excitement generated will be stimulating, and will increase their motivation to discover and achieve in other settings.

# PROVIDING POSITIVE REINFORCEMENT DEVELOPS POSITIVE ATTITUDES

Parents who are effective in motivating children offer suggestions and give directions in a positive manner. By showing children or helping them learn *how* to do a task and *how* to be successful, you can help them learn to solve problems and complete tasks. The goal setting techniques discussed in Chapter 5 will be convenient ways to assist your child in becoming successful.

Stating directions and suggestions positively helps children know that a task or challenge can be accomplished. In this way, they know what can be done. Positive comments aid in building a good self-concept and provide help and encouragement in tackling more difficult challenges. Comments such as "That's a good start, let's try again" help to encourage children to continue trying after they have failed, and emphasize the importance of their efforts despite mistakes along the way. On the other hand, comments such as "That is wrong" or "Oops, missed again" do little to improve a person's self-concept or to motivate him or her to try again.

By using positive comments, you provide positive reinforcement which increases the possibility that a task or challenge will be repeated. These comments include the verbal encouragement that is given, such as "Nice try," or "I bet if you stack those blocks nice and straight you can get five to stay up in your stack." In this case the reinforcement is positive and helpful.

It is easy to provide positive reinforcement when your child shows progress toward a goal or reaches a goal. However, it is not as easy to help your child deal with failures and especially to learn to deal with them in a positive way. Children must be helped to realize that an error is a way of learning and not just a mistake. By showing your child the correct way to do something, by helping him or her to understand where the mistake was made, and how to improve the performance, he or she can gain a new perspective in approaching the task more positively.

Problem-solving approaches can be beneficial to your child when a mistake is made. It is necessary that a new solution to a problem be discovered. You can assist in this problem-solving venture. You can ask questions or suggest new challenges. Your child will then gain confidence in his or her ability to solve problems or overcome mistakes.

# LEARNING TO "DO YOUR BEST" IS IMPORTANT

Your positive approach is important as you motivate your child. As children learn to set goals and work toward them, they learn to challenge themselves. Another way to motivate your child includes learning to compete against some standard or against another child. Caution must be taken in introducing this type of competition before your child has enough confidence in his or her own abilities. Competition with a good chance to be successful is very healthy.

You should place importance on competing with yourself as opposed to competing with others. The focus of all competition should be on skill development rather than beating an opponent. In this light your child is, in fact, attempting to accomplish successive goals by competing against past performances, thus raising his or her own standards.

# SERVING AS A ROLE MODEL

Children are quick to copy the actions and attitudes of their parents. Therefore, you must be aware of the model that you are presenting for your child to follow. In doing your job well, you must be a model of the type of person you would like your child to become. For example, if you want your child to strive for success, then you must be seen as someone who strives for success. Your success as an adult, as a parent, and as someone who cares, provides important information for your child.

Your child will observe you and other adults dealing with frustration. You will set an example for children to follow in facing their own frustrations. Adults are not always successful and sometimes even the best effort will not be enough. When your child sees you meet challenges head on, though you may not always accomplish the desired goal, you will demonstrate how you cope with frustration. Frustration does not mean that you or your child give up, but rather that you learn how to handle challenges better in the future.

# KEY CONCEPTS

- Provide an environment for exploration.
- Give directions in a positive manner.
- Use praise for trying to accomplish tasks.
- Help your child be successful.
- Serve as a model for your child.
- Be a model for dealing with frustrations.
- Show your child how to face failure in a positive way.
- Show your child love and support.

## Suggested Reading

Gordon, T. *Parent effectiveness training*. New York: P.H. Wyden, 1970.

# 2
# UNDERSTANDING YOUR CHILD

Key issues to be addressed in this chapter:
- Understanding Total Behavior
- Understanding the Development of Your Child at Each Age Level from 3-8 Years of Age

Understanding how to help your child become the best he or she can be is a major challenge for all parents. Three to eight year olds are complex little people, filled with untapped abilities and skills, and excited about life. Understanding physical, cognitive, and social-emotional development will help you guide your child toward a happier and healthier life. Recognizing physical and cognitive abilities will help you select activities in which your child can happily participate.

Your child's world is one of play and physical activity. A child's social, emotional and cognitive skills are expanded and demonstrated through play. This chapter will describe the characteristics of children three to eight years of age, in terms of *total behavior*. Behavior is complex and points out the interaction of all parts of the child's lives. It is possible to consider each aspect of the child separately, but, the child does not function as separate components.

Some information in this chapter will be discussed in terms of specific ages. This organization is provided merely to show a developmental trend.

You must not assume that your three year old or six year old should be just like the ones described. For example, your three year old child may have shown some of the behaviors at the age of two, while others may not be observed until four or five years old. The important point is to recognize the changing behaviors of each individual child.

# UNDERSTANDING THE DEVELOPMENT OF YOUR CHILD

## • The Three Year Old

Your "former baby" is now a three year old child. Children at three years of age are delightful individuals. Their curiosity is intense and rate of learning is amazing. They have mastered many movements and concepts. Language is beginning to play an important role as the individual identity and uniqueness of each child is emerging.

Physically, the three year old is growing at a slower rate than during the first two years of life and the trunk is just beginning to catch up. The legs are still growing faster than the arms. Children can vary greatly in size and shape. Three year olds will often be 34-43 inches tall with normal weight ranges from 25 to 52 pounds.

The early experiences of childhood have a lifelong effect. Children probably will not remember many experiences and lack words to give these experiences shape but the feelings will remain. Your child needs to continue to receive warm support and love. If you push too fast, a lack of confidence may develop. You must continue to help your child expand his or her world and leave babyhood behind. Help your child feel confident and secure. You must show that you have faith. Allow some trial and error learning.

Most three year olds can catch a ball with arms held out straight, build towers and construct bridges with many blocks. Most can button and unbutton clothing, put on shoes, balance on one foot, and walk upstairs. Jumping and climbing are also natural results of increasing curiosity and added strength. Lines and circles can be drawn and simple figures copied.

Children are wonderfully expressive. They love to play with sounds. The nonsense talk, or "ga,ga, zoom, boom, gaggle, girgle, giggle," helps in the mastery of language. A good rhythm of nonsense words can keep a group of pre-schoolers marching around for hours.

This unconscious need to master language and to be independent creates some difficult times. Language can be a powerful tool for your child. It might cause you to laugh or be shocked. The sudden discovery of "wee wee" or "pee" or other less desirable words are exciting to children. If you ignore this play or substitute your own nonsense words, you can usually avoid problems and join in the delight of words.

Words and rhythms are wonderful tools for play. Singing games, finger plays, nursery rhymes, and dances will delight your child plus help language skills. Let your child help create rhymes and dances. Build some homemade musical instruments out of bottle caps, sand paper blocks, or pots and pans for your own family band.

Preschoolers experience many problems and frustrations. Most of these problems come from natural changes in bodies and minds. Your child is very curious so many things get taken apart. This seems especially true with increasing independence. It may even disrupt daily routines. Naps, dressing, and eating seem to be very frustrating for all as we help the three year olds. After all, you are getting in the way of important things—play and people.

The curiosity of your child can often lead to cuts and scrapes. He or she may fall off beds, tumble down stairs, get cut on broken glass, or skin knees. These "growing pains" are important for the child. You must instill caution but not fear. Through a fair amount of experience with pain, sharpness, heat, and cold, decisions will be made and a healthy fear of unsafe things will develop.

Children may show physical signs of tension or frustration such as thumbsucking, eye blinking, or nail biting. Vivid imaginations may often lead to nightmares and make-believe friends. These friends are quite common, seem quite real, and may even require an extra cookie, hug or kiss!

Socially, three year olds are eager to try new experiences, but still need protective guidance. This is the prime age for your child to gain self-confidence and a desire to try new things. The preschooler can cooperate for a limited time and is learning to take turns. Parallel play situations can be seen as your child plays in a common location with other children, but does not play with others. Preschoolers tend to play best alone since sharing of equipment is not generally understood and cooperation is difficult. This suggests that adult guidance must be very subtle, as children must learn to do things for themselves. Resentment may sometimes occur if an adult interferes in the play situation.

Helping children feel good about themselves is an important step at this age. The new experiences of a three year old are chances to develop an "I can do it" attitude, rather than an "I can't do it" attitude. The sense of mastery, communicated by "watch me," is essential at this age. Parents need to be there to watch and approve.

Constant encouragement is necessary. Fears of the unknown, fears of heights or of falling are common and are often learned from fearful adults. Such fears are learned; they can be overcome by successful experiences. The desire to gain approval is great and praise and encouragement are welcomed.

# • The Four Year Old

Four year old children are quite remarkable. The physical coordination of four year olds is much more advanced than three year olds. Height has doubled since birth; their arms and legs are stronger and allow for faster and smoother runs and throws. Children can walk on a balance beam, gallop, and even jump well if given the chance to learn. When given plenty of space, they will run with sheer joy and imitate whatever adults are doing, from washing the car or floor, to playing pretend tennis games.

Fine motor skills are also advancing. Many children are able to make crude designs and letters, color in figures, and cut on a line with scissors. Dressing independently and personal toileting are progressing at this age.

Children between three and four years of age are beginning to develop many motor skills. Basic skills of throwing and catching, running, jumping, and skipping will be observed if the child is given the appropriate experiences. The motor patterns of your child at this level tend to reflect the types of opportunities provided.

Getting along with others becomes a key aspect of the years between three and four. Children learn a great deal by imitating the actions of peers and by trying to do what others can. Children need to play with other children, even though four year olds do not always play well with others. Social skills are developing rapidly at this age, and motor skills will also continue to improve if children are given opportunities to play with others.

Socially, four year olds begin to enjoy playing in groups of two or three children. Learning to share and be aware of the opinions and rights of others is becoming evident. Play experiences can help the child develop socially. Story plays, dress-up, and role playing help the child learn about others, while simple games allow for sharing and cooperation.

Children need to do lots of testing and exploring. The four year old loves to hammer, pound, twist, bounce, and roll objects. Objects are stacked only to be knocked over on purpose. Open spaces are needed in which to run and throw; obstacles are needed to climb on, over, and in. The environment should be filled with stimulating items and freedom of choice.

Your child can benefit from a group setting if mature enough to be away from familiar surroundings. If your child is not ready for long periods of play with other children, he or she may need to stay where more individual attention can be received. A good setting is one which provides lots of play space, other children with whom to play, and a wide variety of activities. It should be a warm and supportive environment in which your child is encouraged to try new things and strive to do more or better with each effort.

Many three and four year olds attend some organized form of school or play group. A setting geared to the special interests or needs of your child should be selected. Environments vary greatly. Parents should visit and observe both the adults and children before selecting a school.

The increased use of imagination can be seen in the play of the child. It can sometimes even override reality as imaginary friends become playmates or blocks of wood and pieces of clay become trucks or railroad trains. Children gain experience and learn how it feels to be something or someone else. There may be difficulty in keeping truth and fiction separate as imagination and curiosity continue to develop.

Infants and toddlers are often afraid of real things. However, the imagination of some four year olds is a problem. Everyday situations may now be frightful such as being carried on your shoulders, or standing on the couch. The vacuum may have been fun to run a few months ago but now he or she screams at the sound. Cuts and scrapes may now seem like major disasters and always require a bandage. Such fears are probably part of growing up. Four year olds want to know everything and to be able to control things. A lack of power and control often leads to fear and frustration. Broken toys are major problems, though not always because they don't work, but rather because they cannot be the same as they were.

You can help overcome these fears by showing children that you can control some things but not others. You can give support and encouragement as your child explores the world. Show how you deal with fear by gathering information and cautiously uncovering the unknown. You may have to help in the rediscovery of the fun of riding on your shoulders, climbing the slide, or turning on the vacuum.

The physical abilities of children are improving rapidly at this age. Your child will be more adventurous and daring in running, jumping, and climbing, and want to explore everything. Movements should be purposeful—to get somewhere or something. Play can also be used to "be something or somebody." Children are "trying on" different roles such as the garbage collector, postal carrier, mother, father, secretary, doctor, bus driver, engineer, carpenter, nurse, etc. Almost anything in sight can be used for play. Leaves, bottle caps, and dandelions make great tea parties. A piece of cloth can be a hat, queen's robe, or carpenter's apron. A rope might be a fire fighter's hose, missile, snake, lasso, or necklace.

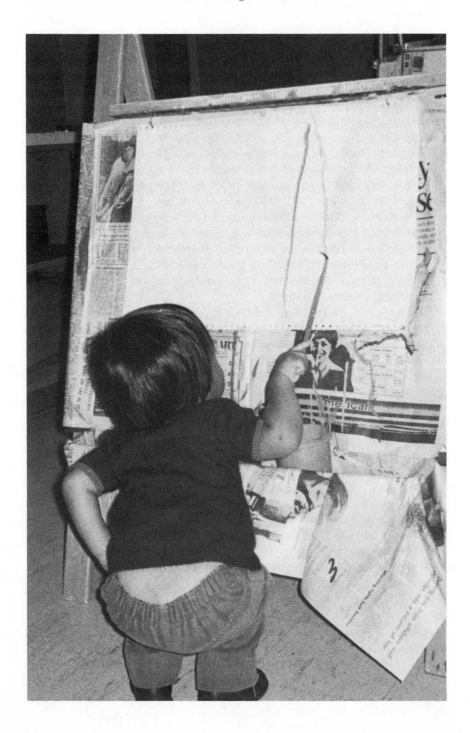

The imagination of children can be expressed through many play activities. When allowed to explore with crayons, finger paints, sand, water, mud, and clay, children continue to develop fine motor skills as the imagination is allowed to be expressed.

The increasing development of fine motor skills is both a blessing and a problem causer. The use of spoons and forks helps children gain independence in eating but as more skill is developed attention is easily distracted. When coupled with increased social skills and a desire to talk to you, there may be many eating accidents and spilled milk. This is only natural since once a skill can be easily done, it may no longer require as much concentration.

Experiences must be provided which allow challenges to be accepted and met head on, yet give a sense of what to expect. As self-sufficiency and independence are learned, attempts and efforts at solving problems must be reinforced to a greater extent than the actual accomplishment. It is the *process,* or the desire to learn and attempt challenges, that is much more important than the actual results.

It is critical for you to establish an atmosphere of freedom and encouragement. The tone which is set will determine the amount of freedom and responsibility fostered in your child. The young child who is confined and overprotected will not grow into an independent, self-reliant adult.

# • The Five Year Old

The characteristics of the five year old mark the completion of early childhood. The growth rate is slower, with height increasing more than weight. Legs which have grown quickly often cause the child to have a top-heavy appearance. The knock knees and protruding tummies of earlier years are disappearing. Children vary tremendously in size and ability because growth and maturation rates can be quite different from one child to another.

The fine motor skills of five year olds are more mature. Designs, numbers, and letters can be copied more easily. Because the child may be farsighted, long periods of close work on crafts will not be met with great success. Complex block structures are being built. Nearly independent dressing and good table manners are evident. There is a fascination with puzzles, assembling and taking things apart. Help may be needed with these activities, though some children will also resent interference as a struggle for independence is seen.

Large motor skills are still more easily controlled and better developed than fine motor skills. Activities might include climbing ladders and jungle gyms, walking backward on a straight line, or hopping several times on one foot. Throwing and catching will be getting better. A wide variety of opportunities should be provided to aid in the development of physical skills and a sense of self-confidence.

Most five year olds prefer one hand over the other. Many children have switched hands several times between two and five years and may still not have a clearly preferred hand or eye. Because the preference for one side over the other seems to be a basic part of each individual's make-up, your child should be allowed to show a natural preference. In early years, selection will be facilitated if you present objects in the middle and allow the child to reach for them. Observe which hand is most often used. Once a clear preference is shown, encourage its use by placing objects on that side of the child. You may also wish to remind your child to "use your favorite or best hand." The important point is to help one side to develop better than the other. Children who constantly switch hands will have difficulty in more advanced behaviors.

Five year olds are becoming real social beings. There is a definite personality that can be dealt with on a more mature level. Curiosity and lots of questions are common. The "what ifs" and "how comes" are essential for social and mental growth, even if they are tiresome to you! Sorting out what is real from what is make-believe is important as children of this age learn to listen and understand.

29

Many five year olds are beginning their first school or away from home experience. In order to feel happy and confident your child must be ready for the new independent experience. Following directions and getting along with others is very important. Children of this age may be quite noisy, active, and boisterous, though they still tire easily.

The need to explore physical potential is even more marked at this age. Most children are also learning to get along with peers. Children at this age are therefore interested in play and games which help in identifying individual roles.

Friends are generally chosen because of similar interests and abilities. Afternoons can be filled with friends on big wheels or two wheelers, in games of four square, elastic jump rope, soccer, or "war." They like other children who have ideas like their own. This often creates problems in small groups where "three's a crowd" seems all too true. These children seem to do best with one other friend or a group of four or more.

Five year olds are much more aware of their world. Double-checks are made on what others may think. Sometimes it is important to consider what friends would do or think as opposed to parents or other adults. Play next door, or down the street, may be chosen but your child may come home periodically just to check. There is often a mixed need for support and independence.

Understanding how things work and doing things right are important at this age. Using "real" things and following the rules are important. Children begin to like crafts from which real or useable objects result. Baking and building, helping in the garden, and beginning to play musical instruments are enjoyed.

Rules can be quite important—sometimes too important. Children may be overly demanding of themselves and others. The tattletale stage often emerges as children expect everyone to "play by the rules". You often hear "that's not fair...," "you said I could..." or "why shouldn't I do it" when something seems unfair to the child. Telling tales or complaining about guidelines or requirements may merely reflect the child's own concern for living up to the rules.

# • The Six Year Old

As children enter first grade, baby fat is gradually lost and signs of more adult-like bodies are seen. Trunks gain size so that arms and legs no longer appear so long. Physical stamina increases, and when tired, recovery is quick.

Motor skills continue to advance quickly, with large motor skills being better than fine motor skills. Children are developing good visual skills as can be seen by improved throwing, kicking, and catching. The visual system, the eye itself, is almost its full size and with this maturity comes the ability to focus on closer objects. This is a marked improvement over the farsightedness of earlier years.

Six year olds should have developed all of the basic locomotor skills: walking, running, leaping, hopping, galloping, sliding, and skipping. In addition, most children will be able to throw and catch a ball, although large differences between children can be observed. Many of these differences are the result of different experiences provided by parents and teachers, brothers, sisters, and friends.

Most children of this age love to move, especially to music. Rhythm can be kept to the beat of a drum or march. Simple dance games are enjoyable and should be encouraged as a way to develop creativity and free expression. It is important that both boys and girls be allowed to try all types of activities.

Girls should be allowed to build with objects and play roughhouse or large motor games. Similarly, boys should be encouraged to dance, play house, sweep, and participate in a full range of activities.

Children can vary greatly in size and shape by six years of age. Boys and girls grow at uneven rates through the first ten years. Girls tend to be slightly more mature than boys in terms of physical development. This becomes especially obvious between six and ten years of age when girls may be one to two growth years ahead of boys. This gives many girls an advantage in controlling motor skills such as learning to write, dress, and handle implements.

Children of this age are eager adventurers. They believe that anything can be conquered, yet most of them will need help with the unknown.

You may believe that you know and understand your six year old, only to be surprised by new behaviors. Your child is a very complex human being. Each child's personality is made up of many facets, but like everyone, requires:

► A chance to be loved;
► Food, sleep, air, shelter, and protection;
► The opportunity to be unique and independent;
► Freedom to grow—mentally, physically, and emotionally.

# • The Seven Year Old

Seven year olds are active, curious beings. Increasing physical skills make it possible to do many things, particularly as attention span increases from earlier years. There is a need to be challenged and to demonstrate capabilities.

The physical skills of your child are developing rapidly. Hand-eye and perceptual motor abilities allow for jumping rope, riding bicycles, and beginning to play a variety of activities.

Fine motor skills are also developing to the point of being able to print and write, color, draw simple figures, cut, and paste. Interests in cooking, sewing, and building things begin to appear. Crafts and art projects are ideal for sparking these interests and helping your child to develop new skills.

Seven year olds are generally more self-directed and less impulsive. Acting independently and demonstrating skills are important. There is a need to know how everything works, sometimes with almost uncontrolled curiosity. Your child will be creative when there is freedom to explore, to experiment, or to try new things. Many and varied interests will develop if the child is given opportunities to try a variety of activities.

Though attention spans are longer than a year ago, your seven year old still requires exciting and stimulating environments. Your child's play areas should be full of objects to manipulate, not necessarily expensive toys, but a wide variety of objects. These toys might range from pots and pans to boards and blocks, to grown-up clothes for dress up.

New skills and abilities fascinate children. The same action may be repeated over and over again. Getting on and off a bicycle can be done at least twenty different ways. Moving rapidly is quite important to your child; scooters, wagons, big-wheels, roller skates, and skate boards take on new importance.

Counting games and routines are popular. Riddles and "corny" jokes are also ways to practice language. Rituals are important, like wishing on a star, kicking cans, and jumping cracks to avoid "breaking your mother's back." Family routines are also important. Bedtime stories before bed, or always brushing teeth right after breakfast may be very important because they are stable and predictable occurrences.

Socially, seven year olds are becoming more interested in group activities. There is fascination with problems to solve and organized game activities. This is the time for stressing the importance of rules and fair play. Children of this age are generally honest and truthful and learn to respect other's rights.

Children learn at very different rates. A particular child may easily learn to skip or bat a ball, but have a very difficult time with a pencil or scissors. Your child may find making a bed "conveniently" difficult, but roller skating or building sand castles easy. These early differences tell you about the child as an individual. They should not be used to predict eventual skills or abilities. It is too early to decide what can or cannot be learned. Be patient and supportive.

Your youngster is a traveler, in and out of childhood. The trip away from the security of home leads into an independent world. Your child must grow to be strong and brave, as the environment is discovered and as individual abilities and skills emerge.

As children grow to be more self-confident, fears are faced and conquered. Some fears are healthy such as the hazards of cars and trucks, fire, water, and electricity. These dangers are no less "real" than the fear of not being loved or accepted, or not being able to be as good as an older sister or brother, or mom or dad. Fears are overcome as your child learns to be self-sufficient and knows that you will help. A few successful conquests and small victories over real or imaginary obstacles help to shape confidence.

# • The Eight Year Old

Physical growth and development continue to proceed at a rather steady rate for eight year olds, except for a few children, usually girls, who may show a growth spurt. This is a good age for checking locomotor and postural skills for potential problems.

Eight year olds are becoming more mature in seeking to know who, what, when, where, and how. Less emphasis on self is seen than in the younger children, and more interest in playing with others can be observed. Motor skills are improving, and the desire to really learn how to throw and catch make this an ideal age. Some children at this age will actively practice skills for the sake of improving and enjoy the challenge of "doing better."

Primary aged children are in a constant state of change. Mood and interests change rapidly. One moment they may want to argue and be assertive and then suddenly cooperative and loving. Your understanding will be needed as discovery is made about what they are capable of doing.

Adult approval continues to be very important at this age. A newfound peer group or "gang life" is beginning to emerge. Working together is beginning to appear in games and other activities. Your child may still want to be the star and score the goal but now sees the reason for passing the ball. Cooperation is ideally taught at this age, especially when coupled with discussion about "doing your best," winning, losing, and good team play.

Eight year olds are developing self-portraits which are formed by past experiences. One child may imagine being the smart, strong athlete, while another might imagine being a naughty boy who is always blamed for everything. Some might think of being the brave girl who will be the first to the top of the tree, the clever artist, or perhaps only the cute child with curly hair. The self-concept which is developing will continue to be shaped. Your child needs a positive, good feeling and self-picture.

Children need to be individuals. A strong need for privacy and control may show itself at this age. The desire for a pet may be one demonstration of this need to be an adult and to help something or someone else. Work and play projects should be encouraged. This helps develop independence and responsibility.

Life is one large experiment as everything seems to be taken apart. Hobbies, pets, and collections of almost endless variety emerge. Some interests are short-lived while others may become lifelong hobbies.

Projects should include a great deal of variety. Some should be hard while others easily completed. Mistakes at this age are easily overcome and make little difference. Children must learn to try hard and also to know when to quit if a job is beyond reach. A few stumbling blocks are good, especially if most of them can be overcome by trying hard or attempting a new solution.

# KEY CONCEPTS

Understand Your Child and His or Her Unique:

- Physical abilities
- Mental capabilities
- Social and emotional needs

Help Your Child To Be Happy and Healthy By:

- Being understanding
- Being supportive and loving them
- By challenging them to do their best

## Suggested Readings

Bijou, S.W. *Child Development: The Basic Stages of Childhood*. Engelwood Cliffs, N.J.: Prentice-Hall, 1976.

Butler, A.L., Gotts, E.E. and Quisenberry, N.L. *Play as Development*. Columbus: Charles E. Merrill, 1978.

Carro, G. How to raise a brighter baby: Learning is a child's play. *Ladies Home Journal*, July, 1978, p. 60.

Greenberg, S. *Right from the Start: A Guide to Nonsexist Child Rearing*. Boston: Houghton Mifflin Co., 1979.

Lever, J. Child's play: What every parent needs to know. *Ms.*, Fall, 1977, p. 22.

Matterson, E.M. *Play and Play Things for the Preschool Child*. Baltimore: Penguin Books, 1978.

Piers, M.W. and Helstein, T.J. Play: The key to educational growth. *Parents' Magazine*, November, 1977, p. 67.

Sutton-Smith, B. and Sutton-Smith, S. *How to Play with Your Children (And When Not To)*. New York: Hawthorne, 1974.

Weissbound, B. Playfulness spurs development. *Parents*, September, 1979, p. 70.

# 3
# THE IMPORTANCE
# OF PLAY

Key issues to be addressed in this chapter:

- Understanding the Importance of Play
- Becoming Aware of the Importance of Parental Attitudes
- Developing an Interest in Play
- Realizing the Differences in the Play of Children
- Recognizing the Types of Play and Games
- Types of Play
- Appreciating that Variety is Important

## UNDERSTANDING THE
## IMPORTANCE OF PLAY

Play is perhaps the most important part of your child's life. In the early years children must use movement to learn about their world. They move to learn. They like to put things together, take things apart, move things from place to place, or just move themselves. These challenges help develop their self-concepts and a sense of "who I am."

Play activities provide opportunities for your child to learn to feel confident about his or her abilities. If children are encouraged to attempt move-

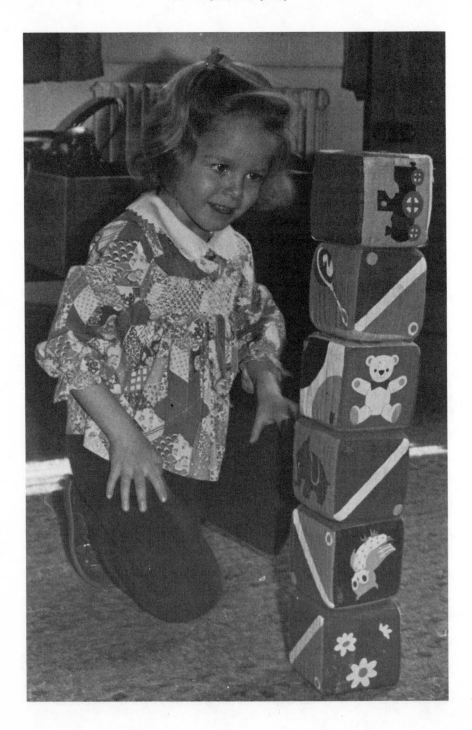

ment tasks, such as bouncing a ball ten times in a row today and then working toward twenty times by next week, they learn to set goals and to work toward them. This teaches the value of hard work and practice. Then when the goal is reached they feel good about themselves.

Movement provides a way in which children explore capabilities, and learn about themselves and their environment. Every child must be allowed to explore his or her abilities and to learn to solve problems. Through play and games, children can learn who they are and what they are capable of becoming.

Prior to school, your child is at an age of exploration which is important for development. It is often a very frustrating time for you since your child may be getting into everything. They love to explore each object—to push, twist, and bang. While this might be a trying time for you these are important experiences for your child.

The years from two until school age are the years in which most basic movement patterns are established. It is important that your child be exposed to a wide range of activities which require small or fine movements and large motor activities such as throwing, catching, kicking, and running. It is important that adults participate with the child at this time. As an adult you serve as a model for your child's performance, someone to praise effort and someone to encourage continued exploration. In addition, your child will share the pleasure you find in play by observing your enthusiasm and fun.

# BECOMING AWARE OF THE IMPORTANCE OF PARENTAL ATTITUDES

Play is a useful tool in the development of your child. It can aid in your child's growth toward becoming a more social being. Play offers your child a unique opportunity for combining various experiences to form opinions and ideas and to grow as an individual. It is the role of the adult to assist in the selection of play activities in such a way that learning can take place.

Understanding the importance of play is critical for parents. If your child is to have a wide range of play and work choices, you must provide a broad base of early skills. This should include the development of good movement skills and fundamental movement patterns during the preschool years.

The total amount of time you spend playing with your child is probably not nearly as important as the quality of time spent in play. It is not even critical that all the play be provided by parents—other children, aunts and uncles will all help. The establishment of this warm, loving environment will help the child's motor development, self-concept, and feelings of security. The new experiences of childhood provide a key element in early play. Children must discover how to use their bodies. This becomes a major goal for play during the early years of life.

Early movement experiences are critical for the development of all children. However, play should be matched with the needs and ability level of the child. Playing with children does not involve forcing participation but rather going along as interests develop. Changes should be made to account for varied ability levels and interests. It is important to help children enjoy play through encouragement and even imitation. Regardless of the situation, play encourages the child to explore the environment and expand movement capabilities.

Your role in helping your child learn to excel is very important. Your child looks toward you for encouragement and guidance. Unfortunately, adults can also bias a child's play by the type of comments made. For example, parents may say "Boys will be boys" and accept the fact that they may get dirty. On the other hand, when a girl gets dirty, a comment like "Oh, your clothes got dirty, let's brush them off," may indicate to that child that she should not be playing an activity in which she will get her clothes dirty. If you make the same comment for both your son and daughter, the comment is not as likely to influence the play choices of your child for a particular activity.

Free expression is important through the play activities of your child. Both boys and girls should be seen as individuals growing and discovering the world. You must allow for this growth and be willing to put aside such personal feelings as "Boys don't cry" or "Girls don't wrestle or perspire."

During the preschool years children are beginning to develop all of their motor skills. The beginning skills of throwing, catching, running, jumping, and skipping are developing. The motor patterns of children at this level tend to reflect the types of opportunities they have had. Children whose parents have spent great amounts of time praising their fine-motor skills, such as drawing, painting, building with blocks, etc., will show competence and interest in these areas. Similarly, if enough time has been spent running, jumping, and playing catch with your child, interests and desires in these areas will be developing as well.

Playing with others becomes important in the early years. Your child learns a great deal by imitating the actions of peers and by trying to do what others can. Social skills are developing rapidly, and motor skill development can be helped if given a chance to play with others.

# DEVELOPING AN INTEREST IN PLAY

How can you develop an interest in play? Participate in it yourself. Do not simply talk about it or ask "What do you want to do?" Encourage your child's participation by setting a good example. Understanding that your child will "do as you do" must guide your actions. Exciting parents pull from in front, and do not push from behind.

Helping children learn from play requires a fine balance between keeping them motivated and giving them enough specific information at the right time to affect learning. Several suggestions may be helpful in structuring your comments to your child. Specifically, try to be:

► CONSTRUCTIVE not destructive
► POSITIVE not negative
► SPECIFIC not general
► SOONER not later

*Constructive* comments to children help them see positive aspects of their performance and build on this. You should deal with observable behaviors so that your child knows how to do better. For example, you may wish to tell your child that his or her house of ten blocks looks great—"Can you add two more?" What a difference from the parent who merely comments, "Can't you use twelve blocks?"

The positive comments you make do two different things. They reinforce something that can be built upon and they praise the child. Similarly, the more *specific* your comments can be, the better your child can determine what should be, instead of what is. You must let your child feel accepted and feel that his or her play will also be accepted. Your child learns through play and you can best help this learning by encouraging your child to explore the world.

Parents should keep track of play activities and re-direct them if they prove to be harmful or otherwise damaging to the child's well-being. Parents must provide this direction when it is needed. Often children will not realize the consequences of their play behaviors and how these behaviors may affect another child. In this type of situation a gentle guiding hand by a parent can and should be used.

As you play with your child you either consciously or unconsciously affect his or her behavior. In order to help your child experience different play activities, he or she should be encouraged in a variety of ways. Take a moment to fill out the following "Adult Checklist."

# ADULT CHECKLIST FOR CHILDREN'S PLAY

| When you work with children, do you emphasize: | Always | Sometimes | Never |
|---|---|---|---|
| 1. working together to accomplish goals? | | | |
| 2. play with both same sex and opposite sex children? | | | |
| 3. respect for others and fair play? | | | |
| 4. problem-solving? | | | |
| 5. assertiveness in both boys and girls? | | | |
| 6. competitiveness when appropriate? | | | |
| 7. team functioning and cooperation when appropriate? | | | |
| 8. tolerance for the less skilled? | | | |
| 9. following rules? | | | |
| 10. individual initiative? | | | |
| 11. similar expectations for both boys and girls? | | | |
| 12. that both boys and girls help with equipment? | | | |
| 13. equal access to all play activities? | | | |
| 14. role models of both sexes in all activities? | | | |
| 15. equal caution and safety by·both boys and girls? | | | |
| 16. creative expression of feelings and ideas? | | | |
| 17. inventiveness and creativity? | | | |
| 18. rules and strategy? | | | |
| 19. independence? | | | |
| 20. completing projects or activities? | | | |

# REALIZING THE DIFFERENCE
# IN CHILDREN'S PLAY

All children love to be held, but how much? As a parent you may play with and hold boys very differently than girls. Sometimes boys are not held as much as girls, and some adults tend to be much more playful with boys than with girls. Girls are sometimes sheltered and protected more than boys since parents think that boys will later protect these same girls. But what happens to the girl when there is no one to protect her, or to the boys or girls who become single parents, or decide never to have families of their own? All children should be given equal opportunities to be held, loved and to learn to be independent.

Differences occur during early infancy as a result of different parenting practices for children. For example, children who are likely to become high achievers, traditionally males, are often allowed to play a greater distance from parents and are taught to be more independent at an earlier age. High achievers are also seen playing in larger groups and they learn to choose competitive experiences. Such children eventually show more and more confidence toward attempting difficult tasks, with more confidence and patience in getting them finished. Children who are encouraged to play indoors or close to home, to play cooperative games in small groups, and to play in activities where winning and/or losing are not seen to be important, may develop into adults who have low desires to achieve.

Children raised with a full range of play choices will develop skills and attitudes necessary to achieve closer to their potential. This equality of opportunity for all children is critical to the development of achievement abilities necessary in adulthood.

Each activity is simply another way to learn to grow and to have fun. Free expression is necessary. Materials should not be seen as having one use and one use only. To be creative and imaginative the child must be able to visualize different uses of material. Blocks, dress-up and pretend all have their place in each child's play and should be encouraged for both sexes. The idea of activities being "boy" or "girl" must be overcome. Children do not label activities as such until adults suggest that such a difference exists.

Parents often worry about the way their child plays. A girl who enjoys building things, repairing things, or working hard physically is sometimes labeled a "tomboy," while a boy who enjoys cooking and sewing may be labeled a "sissy." Yet we know that children should be allowed to consider all types of activities which may help them meet future needs or demands. If girls can become surgeons, carpenters, lawyers, or athletes when they grow up, then they must be allowed to try these early roles as children. Boys must learn the skills to choose to be a tailor, chef, or father. All children must experience a wide range of activities so that they will feel free to choose for themselves when the time comes to choose.

The typical classroom includes activity areas for building, housekeeping, dress-up, and large motor skills. At home, children can also be given opportunities to involve themselves in these same kinds of activities. It is important that both boys and girls be allowed to try all types of activities. Girls should be allowed to build things and play competitive games. Boys should be allowed to dress up and go to the housekeeping corner. Both boys and girls should be given experiences that represent a full range of activities so that each learns to be independent and capable of working toward a goal.

It is very hard for young children to establish themselves as both leaders and followers. Their desire for approval by both friends and parents is very strong. Because of this conflict, the games which you play with children should provide them with the opportunity to change leadership positions. Games such as "Follow-the-Leader," "Simon Says," circle games, and simple games all provide chances to be a leader and follower while also allowing them to explore.

Games and activities in which children act together in unison and in cooperative ways such as singing and dancing provide ways to gain movement skills as well as a sense of social belonging. Games such as "Ring around the Rosie," "The Farmer in the Dell," "Here we go round the Mulberry Bush," and "London Bridge" all provide such experiences.

Many activities and games have in the past been linked to the play of either boys or girls. On the next page, indicate your feeling about various activities.

# SELF AWARENESS OF PLAY ACTIVITIES

Place an X in the box if you think the activity is only a boys' activity, or only a girls' activity, or an activity for both boys and girls. There are no right or wrong answers, simply indicate what you think.

| | Boys Only | Girls Only | Both Boys and Girls |
|---|---|---|---|
| Bicycling | | | |
| Cartwheels | | | |
| Climbing Apparatus or Climbing Trees | | | |
| Gymnastics | | | |
| Jump Rope | | | |
| Jacks | | | |
| Dolls | | | |
| Hopscotch | | | |
| Rollerskating | | | |
| Legos® and Lincoln Logs® | | | |
| Folk Dance | | | |
| Dodgeball or Bombardment | | | |
| Ballet | | | |
| Carpenter's Bench | | | |
| Electric Trains | | | |
| Tag | | | |
| Soccer | | | |
| Housekeeping Corner | | | |
| Dress-up | | | |
| Creative Dance to Music | | | |

Take a moment to consider the activities you checked on the "Self Awareness" chart. Are there really reasons for these to be classified as either appropriate for males or for females only? Probably not. Boys need to learn the skills associated with such activities as caring for a baby doll, while girls need experiences with the constructive play of carpentry.

# RECOGNIZING THE TYPES OF PLAY AND GAMES

As a concerned parent, you must be prepared to observe children in play, and determine the value of play. There are many forms of play including: (1) those which foster creativity and an understanding of beauty and (2) those which encourage a desire to do one's best and to achieve. This book concentrates on those forms of play which will help your child learn to try harder under all circumstances.

Your child should be exposed to many types of play activities. At times playing by oneself is more beneficial to the specific activity of the child than playing with others. Sometimes your child may fall into a pattern of only playing alone (solitary play) and participate very little in any other type of play. In a case such as this, you should encourage your child to try another type of play even if this means that you must take time to play with the child. Often children do not know how to enter into a group activity and the experience gained through playing with adults may help children develop the ability to join into group activities with peers.

As children grow older they learn to play together. This play may involve playing near another child, though not with that child (parallel play) or it may involve sharing materials or at least interests (associative or cooperative play). At some point, your child will learn to be both independent and friendly. Your child must be able to stand on his or her own feet, and to also cooperate or compete with others.

Types of Play Should Include:

► Solitary Play
► Parallel Play
► Associative or Cooperative Play

By the time your child enters school, organized play, including games, is seen. Organized games rarely appear prior to the age of five or six because of the child's developmental level. However, by the age of five the child can: (1) carry on longer social interactions, both cooperatively and competitively, (2) plan and carry out longer sequences of activities, (3) exercise more self-control and (4) follow directions and conform to a structure such as that of a game.

Games with rules have roots in the early play experiences of children. In early forms of play, your child must learn how to discover the joys of play experiences. As children grow and mature, both physically and mentally, activities also change. Children begin to be involved in more organized forms of play and games.

The types of games children play reflect the values of society. These games can be divided into three types: games of strategy, games of chance, and games of physical skill. Games of strategy such as checkers or cards are organized activities that stress taking a course of action toward an end result. Strategy games may involve proving oneself or taking a risk. Such activities encourage individual decisions. The second category, games of physical skill, is related to activities which encourage hard work and self-reliance. High value is placed on the effort expended to try to attain the goal.

Games of chance depend on luck resulting in little control on the part of the player. These types of games are typical play choices of low achievers. Almost all board games using dice are examples of games of chance.

Types of Games Should Include:

- ► Strategy
- ► Chance
- ► Skill

Games are often characterized by little or no equipment or materials such as in simple tag games or "Steal the Bacon." In both of these examples, and numerous others, the materials may be changed to suit the particular requirement of the game. These materials generally consist of the body, an object, or an implement. The space, amount of individual effort and roles of the players are also open to change. The players may change roles without changing the nature of the game. There is no clearly defined role that each player must perform for the length of the game. (This is in contrast to sports such as baseball where only the pitcher pitches the ball, for example.)

The level of physical challenge is usually quite evident in games, while requirements for strategy or luck are less evident. The elements of competition and cooperation are dependent upon the structure the parent chooses to use. Also, in games, the reactions of parents or other children are important and are often seen as praise or criticism.

In the following chart, play and games are compared. As can be seen in the chart, games involve a greater degree of structure than play. Up until about eight years of age, play in combination with games is commonly used by parents. Regardless of the level, games involve the element of structure. This structure dictates the "what," the "how" and the desired outcome, each of which may be changed. For example, each success or failure brings outcomes. These new outcomes call for new strategy, in turn making the activity more challenging.

A checklist is included on the next few pages to assist you in evaluating the play behavior of your child. You may wish to use this observation tool to help in determining the nature of the activities in which your child participates.

# COMPARISON OF PLAY AND GAMES

| | Play | Games of Low Organization |
|---|---|---|
| Materials | unspecified | modified or improvised |
| Space | no limitations | arbitrary limitations |
| Effort/Time | no limitations | arbitrary limitations |
| Rules | none predetermined | a few which may be changed or modified |
| Well-defined Roles | none specified | some general but may change |
| Level of Challenge<br>• Skill | unspecified | specified basic movement and manipulative skills |
| • Strategy | | arbitrary |
| • Luck | | arbitrary |
| Competitiveness or Cooperation | uncertain and unconsequential | slight but playing is more important than winning or losing |
| Pre-set Goals | no material reward | praise or criticism |

# PLAY CHECKLIST

A. *Type of Play* (Check one):
Does your child....
   _____ 1. Watch others play?
   _____ 2. Play alone?
   _____ 3. Play with the same material as another child but with no interaction? (parallel play)
   _____ 4. Play with other children around a common activity, interests or materials? (associative play)

B. *Characteristics of Play* (Check one):
Does your child....
   _____ 1. Pretend to be someone or something else during play?
   _____ 2. Play to improve motor activity such as throwing, catching, kicking a ball, etc.?
   _____ 3. Have rules that can be changed during the activity?
   _____ 4. Have rules at the start of play that must remain the same during the activity?
   _____ 5. Have a goal to be accomplished during the play?

C. *Interaction* (Check one for each number):
   1. Are the goals of the activity dependent on:
      _____ (a) your child's own actions?
      _____ (b) the actions of someone else?
   2. Is the activity directed by:
      _____ (a) the parent totally?
      _____ (b) both parent and child involvement?
      _____ (c) the child totally?
   3. Is your child actively involved in the play:
      _____ (a) at all times?
      _____ (b) more than 75% of the time?
      _____ (c) more than 50% of the time?
      _____ (d) more than 25% of the time?
      _____ (e) more than 10% of the time?
   4. Does your child....
      _____ (a) work *together* with other children to reach an outcome?
      _____ (b) work *against* children to reach an outcome?
   5. Does your child...
      _____ (a) know the role he or she must play during the activity?
      _____ (b) change the role during the activity?
   6. Does he or she have to take initiative to be included in the activity?
      _____ (a) must take initiative?
      _____ (b) must take *some* initiative?
      _____ (c) no initiative is needed?

D. *Level of Challenge* (Check one):
Is the activity's outcome determined by:
   _____ (a) skill?
   _____ (b) strategy?
   _____ (c) luck?
   _____ (d) skill and strategy?
   _____ (e) skill and luck?
   _____ (f) strategy and luck?
   _____ (g) skill, strategy, and luck?

E. *Level of Activity* (Check one):
Is the space for the activity:
   _____ (a) free within boundaries?
   _____ (b) very restricted within a limited area?

# APPRECIATING THAT VARIETY
# IS IMPORTANT

Your child should be given a variety of experiences with his or her friends. It is important in a child's development to learn how to get along with others. This gives your child an opportunity to understand the aspects of cooperation, sharing, and differing points of view. Children cannot grow socially in an environment without other children or adults. Social development is an important aspect of human development that should not be ignored. Children with very limited experiences may be overwhelmed when entering a classroom for the first time. They have no idea how to play with other children or how to get along in this environment. Therefore, children must have opportunities to play with and be with other children.

Variety also applies to the types of play materials or toys available to your child. Children exposed to a variety of objects or activities will have an opportunity to be creative in many different ways. For example, girls are allowed to dress up but many times boys are discouraged from participating in this activity. Dress-up offers a perfect opportunity for the child to take another's point of view; therefore, it is important to both boys and girls.

To summarize these major points, your child's play experiences are limited or expanded by those adults with whom daily contact is made. These adults must give directions to the child's play activities but should be careful not to limit the play experiences of the child because of their own biases. Your child must feel free to be creative and free to express ideas and feeling through action. This can be done through the use of a variety of materials. Your child must also have play experiences with other children to develop into the social being that society encourages.

# TYPES OF PLAY

Children's play can be separated in terms of solitary play, parallel play and associative play. These forms of play tend to be seen in a sequential fashion as children grow and mature.

## EXAMPLES OF SOLITARY PLAY

Solitary play is the first type of play to be seen in children. It involves play by oneself without reference to other children. It begins in early childhood when a child plays in a crib or on the floor. It continues throughout life as individual play is enjoyed.

Examples of solitary play (one child alone) might include:

Fill in examples of solitary play in which your child participates:

building with blocks
doing a puzzle
taking things apart
playing in sandbox
drawing/painting/cutting
playing dress-up
climbing
playing with pots and pans
modeling clay
riding a tricycle or bicycle
playing with a doll
hanging from the monkey
    bars
skipping stones

# EXAMPLES OF PARALLEL PLAY

Parallel play is playing with similar materials as others but not engaging in any interaction. There is no personal exchange between children or others in their environment.

Examples of parallel play (two or more children independently) might include:

Fill in examples of parallel play in which your child engages:

cooking lunch
sewing
running; flying kites
coloring or drawing
playing with their own
    dolls
building with tinker toys,
    blocks, etc.
carpentry activities
roller skating/skate
    boarding
hula hooping
finger painting

# EXAMPLES OF ASSOCIATIVE PLAY

Associative play is defined as play with others that involves social interactions. Play that is loosely organized around a common activity, shared interests and materials.

Examples of associative play (two or more children playing together) might include:

Fill in examples of associative play in which your child engages:

playing house
rhythm instruments
tag; running obstacle
   courses
cops and robbers
squirrel in the tree
British bulldog
dodge ball; red light,
   green light
tea party
partner stunts
jumping rope
playing "jacks" or
   dominoes or pick up
   sticks
playing catch
taffee pull
card games or table games
building sand castles or
   playing in the snow

# KEY CONCEPTS

Help Your Child Play:

- Maximize the play experience
- Encourage independence
- Provide a variety of types of play

Set a Standard:

- Help your child work toward a goal
- Provide opportunities for dealing with both success and failure
- Evaluate your child's play environment

## Suggested Readings

Campbell, D. Play equipment: Making your backyard safe. *Parents,* May, 1980. p. 36

Costello, J. Company of their peers. *Parents,* January, 1981, p. 86.

Costello, J. With cape and crown. *Parents,* March, 1980, p. 83.

Fontana, V.J. Helping your toddler learn through play. *Parents,* May, 1979, p. 78.

Hoover, E.L. Power of play. *Human Behavior,* September, 1978, pp. 14-15.

Muenchow, S. and Seltz, V. How play begins. *Parents,* September, 1980, pp. 60-64.

Sutton-Smith, B. Play isn't just kid stuff. *Parents' Magazine,* September, 1978, pp. 38-39.

Tyler, B. Capturing the play spirit of the child. *Educational Digest,* Fall, 1977, pp. 32-35.

Weissbound, B. Beginnings of friendship (2 year olds). *Parents,* April, 1980, p. 88.

# 4
# UNDERSTANDING ACHIEVEMENT MOTIVATION

Key issues to be addressed in this chapter:

- Understanding Achievement Motivation
- Becoming Aware of Parental Attitudes Toward Achievement Motivation
- Developing Positive Self-Concepts
- Observing Play

Within our society, it is important that each of us strive to do our best, whether in school, at home, or away from home at work. We all must compete against our own standards and those set by society. Therefore, children must learn the value of achievement while they are young. Consider the child who is motivated to do well in school or in physical activity. In both instances, the child is competing or comparing himself or herself against a standard of excellence provided either by the parent, teacher, or perhaps the child. Each individual must learn that challenging oneself is the best road to success. It is therefore important to teach children how to set standards that can be reached successfully. It is also important to teach them to deal with failure. The end result will be a child who takes pride in work and accomplishments.

How can you help your child want to achieve? The motive to achieve does not develop the same way in everyone. These differences in the desire to achieve are a result of cultural influence rather than differences present at birth. These cultural differences and experiences have a great impact on the development of goals.

The motive to achieve is learned early in life. Through play, your child can learn to be assertive and self-reliant, but activities must be carefully selected to develop achievement motivation. Traditional play activities have developed high achievement motivation in some children and low motivation in others. Therefore, it is important that experiences be identified and carefully planned to develop high levels of achievement motivation during these early years.

Achievement motivation is developed through experiences. These experiences take place in settings where children spend a considerable amount of time during their early years. Play is particularly important to American children, who spend 65% or more of their free time involved in play. Therefore, if the desire to achieve is learned through the social process, the child's world of play is important in bringing about the desired changes in achievement motivation.

The low achiever may be motivated by a desire to avoid failure, so he or she sets either very high or very low goals. Such a child is almost certain to be guaranteed either success or failure. When low achievers fail, they often say that the task was too hard or failure was due to bad luck. If the low achievers succeed, they say that the task was too easy or success was due to pure luck. They almost never take personal responsibility for either success or failure.

Children who have a strong desire to succeed can be characterized by their goals and the way they feel about success or failure. When such children are able to accomplish a task, they learn to attribute that success to their own efforts. These children learn to identify a desired goal and work hard in order to maintain that goal.

# BECOMING AWARE OF PARENTAL ATTITUDES TOWARD ACHIEVEMENT MOTIVATION

How can you help develop achievement motivation in your child?

Achievement motivation can begin to be influenced as early as the age of two years. Parents' general attitudes and personal needs are reflected in child-rearing practices. The orientation you have toward your own accomplishments will influence your behavior toward your child in everyday situations. Typically, parents expect the same degree of hard work in their child as they do of themselves. Unfortunately, this may mean that some parents will have negative attitudes toward achievement and low expectations for the child. Parents must regularly show positive feelings about working hard and the pleasure and excitement of solving problems and finishing tasks.

Parents play a very important role in helping their children strive for success. Parents who exhibit the desired characteristics and strive to meet their own potential, tend to foster this behavior in their children. For example, by using positive reinforcement for completing tasks, parents place importance on succeeding at tasks through step-by-step behaviors.

Parents can help their child develop a desire to succeed. Sometimes parents might unconsciously show different attitudes toward their child as a result of the tasks they assign. For example, if you always ask the same child to dump the trash, you may be unconsciously saying that he or she is only good at menial tasks. Children need to do chores, but be sure the assignment of chores says that you feel they are responsible and capable.

Why are differences sometimes seen in the desire to achieve between young boys and girls? How are these roles and behaviors developed? What or who has the greatest influence on the development of these roles: heredity, parents, teachers, peers, friends, or the media?

Parents have an important role to play in the total development of their child. In fact, even before the baby is born, parents start to develop and mold attitudes. Many times parents really want a boy or really want a girl, and start buying pink or blue baby clothes or footballs or dolls. They may even decorate the nursery or playroom with very typical "girl" items such as lace or flowers, or with "boy" items such as animals or football players. If adults have different expectations for boys than for girls, different values may be placed on certain behaviors. Thus, sex-role stereotypes may begin to develop.

The differences in parents' expectations for their child are often demonstrated in subtle ways. How do you talk to your child? Do you encourage a variety of experiences, or an attempt at many different tasks? Children must be challenged, both by what you say and what you provide. The following self assessment is designed to help you identify attitudes about children. Answer each question as honestly as you can.

# SELF-ASSESSMENT

Indicate the degree to which you agree with the following statements.

| | Strongly Agree | Agree | Disagree | Strongly Disagree |
|---|---|---|---|---|
| 1. Children who are high achievers have more variety in their play. | | | | |
| 2. Children should be able to do several things with the same toy or piece of equipment. | | | | |
| 3. If children start something they should stick with it until it is finished. | | | | |
| 4. Children should finish one task before beginning another. | | | | |
| 5. Parents should help children set goals for their play. | | | | |
| 6. Parents should encourage and reward the effort that their children show. | | | | |
| 7. It is more important to reward the effort than the end product. | | | | |
| 8. Goals should be set that require hard work, but that are not unreasonably difficult. | | | | |
| 9. Children should be encouraged to be independent. | | | | |
| 10. Children should be encouraged to play alone as well as with others. | | | | |

Your responses to the statements in the "Self-Test" reflect your attitudes toward achieving. Each of the statements would be responded to with "strongly agree" if you are being most effective at helping children learn to value hard work and independence. On the other hand, if you disagreed with any of the statements, you may not be as helpful as possible in assisting children to reach their utmost potential.

As parents, it may be helpful for you to consider carefully the types of play activities in which your children participate. One effective way to check your children and their "achieving" play would be to take ten minutes each day to observe the type of activity and the number of children playing each activity. In some homes or on some playgrounds, you may see more girls playing some games while boys play others. Ask yourself "why?"

# DEVELOPING POSITIVE SELF-CONCEPTS

Each individual must develop a self-concept or a personal view of himself or herself. We acquire a sense of who we are, what we are capable of doing, how we look, and of what value we may be. This self-concept comes about as a result of our experiences and the way others treat us. Thus we learn about ourselves by our own actions and by the way we get along with others.

One important key to helping your child develop a good self-concept is to treat each child as a unique individual. Accept your child for what he or she is, as well as what he or she may be capable of becoming. This acceptance requires that you care about your child by helping when you are needed, showing affection and showing genuine concern.

Your child's individual development should be encouraged. If you provide clear and fair rules and discuss your beliefs and values, it will be possible for your child to function freely within these defined limits. With this approach your child will be able to test his or her own skills and abilities at making decisions. Your child will learn to be a competent human being.

Helping your child develop a healthy self-concept is perhaps the key to fostering happy, successful adults. If you can provide your child with experiences that encourage self-evaluation, not against others, but as a unique human being, your child will be able to accurately and objectively assess personal strengths and weaknesses.

Children thrive on their expanding abilities and welcome praise and encouragement. Such enthusiasm should reflect your values of hard work and skill rather than luck or chance. Your child will learn to value hard work if you also value it.

The achievement behavior of your child is directly related to the degree of positive reinforcement and recognition received from you. Parents who reward independence early are apt to be the ones for whom achievement is personally important. By rewarding your child for hard work and successful achievement, the chance of developing an independent child who feels good about himself or herself will be increased.

# OBSERVING PLAY

Adults who wish to help children develop higher levels of the motivation to work toward excellence must learn to be careful observers. By watching your child's play, it is often possible to learn some very important things. For example, if you observe your child for an hour or two, you may learn a great deal about his or her independence, self-concept, and persistence. Use the checklist entitled "Evaluating Children's Play" to determine what kinds of characteristics your child has while playing.

After you have completed the checklist, take a moment to consider what you have observed. What qualities did you observe? The characteristics in the list represent positive qualities about play and dealing with others. You may wish to take special note of the traits marked with an asterisk (*). These behaviors are especially linked to people who become successful and high in achievement motivation. You should encourage your child to display and value these behaviors.

# EVALUATING CHILDREN'S PLAY

As you work with your child, can he or she be observed:

| | Almost Always | Sometimes | Almost Never |
|---|---|---|---|
| showing recognition to others? | _____ | _____ | _____ |
| displaying independence?* | _____ | _____ | _____ |
| solving problems?* | _____ | _____ | _____ |
| being creative?* | _____ | _____ | _____ |
| showing fear? | _____ | _____ | _____ |
| being dependent or helpless? | _____ | _____ | _____ |
| receiving help? | _____ | _____ | _____ |
| taking risks?* | _____ | _____ | _____ |
| devising new rules?* | _____ | _____ | _____ |
| playing outside of an adult's direct view?* | _____ | _____ | _____ |
| looking for approval from others? | _____ | _____ | _____ |
| motivating himself or herself?* | _____ | _____ | _____ |
| constructing or creating objects?* | _____ | _____ | _____ |
| playing in large open spaces?* | _____ | _____ | _____ |
| cooperating rather than competing? | _____ | _____ | _____ |
| being passive? | _____ | _____ | _____ |

In summary, you are a very important person in the life of your child. Be sure your child feels loved and respected. Everything you do will make a difference in your child's development. You have the opportunity to help your child develop to the greatest potential.

# KEY CONCEPTS

- Helping your child to achieve is important.
- The desire to achieve is learned.
- Praise and encouragement of effort are essential.

## Suggested Readings

Curtis, J. Children vs. your success drive. *Harpers Bazaar,* October, 1977, p. 176.

Kellogg, M. A. Mothers: how they influence your career and your life: Mothers and daughters. *Glamour,* Fall, 1979, pp. 188-190.

Kier, R. J. Expectations of success: Study of children. *Human Behavior,* March, 1978, pp. 24-25.

Pogebrin, L. C. Mothers who raise successful daughters. *Ladies Home Journal,* June, 1979, pp. 31-32.

# ACHIEVEMENT MOTIVATION ACTIVITIES

## *FINE MOTOR (3-5 YEAR OLDS)*

### DRESSING ACTIVITIES

MATERIALS:

zippers

snaps

shoes and shoelaces

cloth with buttons
and buttonholes

ACTIVITIES:

- Button
- Snap
- Hook

- Lace
- Zip
- Tie

KEY POINTS:

→ Encourage and praise the effort put forth. Reinforce the process of accomplishing the task.

# CUT-OUT AND COLORING ACTIVITIES

MATERIALS:

> colored paper
>
> scissors
>
> paste
>
> crayons
>
> simple shapes and designs

ACTIVITIES:

- Trace and color the shapes and designs.
- Cut out shapes and paste to another sheet containing the same design.
- Cut out shapes and make a picture on a separate sheet of paper.

KEY POINTS:

→ Encourage and reinforce the child's skill in sticking with the task until its completion.

# MANIPULATIVE ACTIVITIES

MATERIALS:

> clothespins
>
> plastic bottles

ACTIVITIES:

- Drop clothespins in large-mouth bottle one at a time; use right hand; left hand.
- Drop clothespins in small-mouth bottle using right hand; left hand.
- Increase the distance between hand and bottle, i.e. 1 foot; 2 feet; 3 feet; etc.

KEY POINTS:

→ Stress that the child's ability and effort were responsible for the success. Emphasize sticking with the task until it is completed (persistence training).

# CREATE YOUR OWN ACTIVITIES

MATERIALS NECESSARY:

EXAMPLES OF ACTIVITIES:

KEY POINTS TO BE EMPHASIZED:

→

# *FINE MOTOR (6-8 YEAR OLDS)*

## CUT-OUT ACTIVITIES

MATERIALS:

cut-out materials

scissors

paper

crayons

ACTIVITIES:

- Cut out an outlined circle, square, triangle, etc.
- Cut out a picture you drew.
- Cut out a circle from memory; square; triangle; etc.
- Write your name and cut it out.

KEY POINTS:

→ Emphasize patience in completing the task. Praise the neatness in performing the activity.

# "JACKS"

MATERIALS:

```
"Jacks"

small ball
```

ACTIVITIES:

- Toss ball up, let it bounce once, and catch it in one hand.
- Toss ball up, pick up a jack and catch the ball in same hand after only one bounce; two jacks; three jacks; etc.
- Toss ball up, pick up a jack and place it in the free hand before catching the ball.

KEY POINTS:

→ Praise the effort at following directions and performing the skill to the best of the child's ability. Encourage the child to keep trying until successful, and then praise for continuing to try, or attempting more difficult challenges.

# PICK-UP STICKS

MATERIALS:

```
pick-up sticks
```

ACTIVITIES:

- Pick up 1 stick without moving another stick; 2 sticks; 3 sticks; 4 sticks; etc.
- Pick up sticks of one color such as red or blue, etc. one at a time; 2; 3; 4; etc.

KEY POINTS:

→ Praise the efforts at carefully following the directions and paying attention to the skill at hand.

# DOMINOES

MATERIALS:

```
┌─────────────────────────────────┐
│                                 │
│            dominoes             │
│                                 │
└─────────────────────────────────┘
```

ACTIVITIES:

- Match dots on the dominoes; use right hand; left hand.
- Stack the dominoes so the dots are matched.
- Place all the dominoes standing on one of the long sides.

KEY POINTS:

→ Encourage persistence with the task and the concentration required to complete the task.

# MEASURING ACTIVITIES

MATERIALS:

> measuring cups
>
> sand
>
> dirt
>
> water

ACTIVITIES:

- Stack all the cups inside the largest one.
- Compare measurements using all sizes such as:
  Does the ½ cup hold a cup of sand; etc.?
- How many ¼ cups in a ½ cup; in a cup; etc.?

KEY POINTS:

→ Reinforce the child's ability to follow directions. Encourage the child to actually put the number of measurements into the larger container to reinforce their answers.

# ROPE LETTERS

MATERIALS:

rope (6 ' long)

blackboard and chalk

or

paper and marker

ACTIVITIES:

Write a letter on the board or piece of paper. Challenge the child to recreate the letter with the rope.

- Simple letters (L, T, I)
- Circle letters and numbers (O, 8)
- Combined letters (d, b, B, D)
- Diagonal line letters (N, M, S, Z)

KEY POINTS:

→ Praise the child's efforts at careful watching, making straight lines and good circles.

# CREATIVE PLAY

MATERIALS:

> clay
>
> string
>
> yarn
>
> pipe cleaners

ACTIVITIES:

- Make forms such as circles, triangles, squares.
- Make numbers.
- Make free designs.
- Make large objects; small objects.

KEY POINTS:

→ Compliment the child's selecting of a task and effort at completing it. Reinforce effort and hard work.

# PEG BOARD ACTIVITIES

MATERIALS:

peg board

colored pegs

ACTIVITIES:

- Put large pegs into large holes as quickly as possible.
- Make circles, squares, triangles, etc.
- Outline a picture.
- Use only the right hand to put pegs into board; left hand.
- Use only 2 fingers to put pegs into board; 2 more fingers.

KEY POINTS:

→ Encourage persistence with the task despite any difficulty and reinforce the effort put forth in completing the task.

# CREATE YOUR OWN ACTIVITIES

MATERIALS NECESSARY:

EXAMPLES OF ACTIVITIES:

KEY POINTS TO BE EMPHASIZED:

→

# UNSTRUCTURED PLAY (3-8 YEAR OLDS)

In unstructured play the child is initiating the activity. You are helping to guide your child toward achieving tendencies.

## SANDBOX AND PLAYHOUSE ACTIVITIES

MATERIALS:

```
sandbox

playhouse

shovel

pail
```

ACTIVITIES:

If your child is engaging in these activities, then encourage:

- building a small house with the sand; digging a hole
- planting a garden at your playhouse; in your sandbox
- raking and cutting the grass at your playhouse.

KEY POINTS:

→ Encourage the child to expend effort to complete the task despite success or failure. Reinforce the effort and persistence in finishing the task.

# POT HOLDERS

MATERIALS:

> pot holder frame
>
> multicolored loops

ACTIVITIES:

If your child is engaging in these activities, then encourage:

- making a pot holder
- using 3 colors for the pot holder
- making a design within the pot holder

KEY POINTS:

→ Emphasize patience in completing the task. Praise the neatness of the lacing as well as the final product.

# CREATE YOUR OWN ACTIVITIES

MATERIALS NECESSARY:

EXAMPLES OF ACTIVITIES:

KEY POINTS TO BE EMPHASIZED:

# ORGANIZED PLAY (3-5 YEAR OLDS)

## HOOP ACTIVITIES

MATERIALS:

```
hoops
```

ACTIVITIES:

Movement challenges with hoops can provide ways for children to learn the value of hard work. Examples of challenges might include, Can you...

- whirl your hoop on different parts of your body while walking?
- climb in, out, and around your hoop while keeping your eyes closed?
- roll the hoop as far as possible without it falling over?
- by putting spin on the hoop, throw it and make it come back to you?
- roll the hoop and run through the hoop as it moves?

KEY POINTS:

→ Stress the fact that the child's ability and effort were responsible for success.

# CLAPPING HANDS

MATERIALS:

record player

records

ACTIVITIES:

- Child claps hands to music that has a strong beat, such as a march. Clap loud and then soft. Alternate.
- Child claps hands together, then on knees, then together, etc.
- Play follow-the-leader by clapping on various body parts.

KEY POINTS:

→ Reinforce the child's skill at following directions.

# BEAN BAG TOSS

MATERIALS:

beanbags

decorated boxes
and containers

ACTIVITIES:

Encourage the child to throw a beanbag into a container using an underhand toss. The container can be a box with a clown's face painted on it. The holes in the box for the clown's mouth, eyes or nose can be targets of different sizes (adapted from Fleming, Hamilton, and Hicks, 1977).

• Make sure each child has a beanbag and allow the children to throw all at the same time. Using different color beanbags will allow each child to keep up with his or her beanbags.
• Encourage children to name a target body part and then aim for it.
• Points could be awarded for various hits, or noise makers could be placed in the holes.

KEY POINTS:

→ Praise the skill and hard work it takes to complete the task. Compliment children on choosing one target and practicing until a good toss results.

# HITTING A BALLOON

MATERIALS:

```
balloons
```

ACTIVITIES:

- The child is encouraged to hit a ballon in the air.
- The child keeps the balloon in the air for a specified number of hits or length of time. Count how many hits in a row. Ask the child how many more he or she can do.
- The child assumes various positions while keeping the balloon in the air (i.e. balance on one foot, lying down, etc.).

KEY POINTS:

→ Emphasize persistence with the task and the effort it takes to complete the task.

# JUMPING THE CREEK

MATERIALS:

```
ropes
```

ACTIVITIES:

Form two parallel lines about 1½ to 3 feet apart, depending on the ability of the children. The lines should be long enough to allow the children plenty of room to jump. A child begins along one side of one of the ropes. They are now on a bank, facing the center or creek. On the signal, either "In the Creek" or "On the Bank" the children will attempt to do what is stated. For example, jump between the ropes ("In the Creek") or jump over the ropes ("On the Bank"). After each command the children should be ready for the next command. If the same command is repeated twice the children should not move.

- Use two ropes and vary the distance between the ropes after each round of jumps.
- Place the ropes such that one end of the rope is closer than the other ends. This will allow each child to jump at a point according to his or her ability.

KEY POINTS:

→ Stress the importance of the child's ability to follow directions. Help each child determine his/her own ability level, by selecting a place on the creek which is just wide enough to jump. Encourage the child to try longer jumps as ability develops.

# HIT THE BUCKET

MATERIALS:

> bucket or trash can
>
> balls or beanbags

ACTIVITIES:

Children form a circle around the trash can or bucket. Each child in turn tries to throw the ball into the trash can or bucket. Choose one player to be the retriever. This player must return the ball to the next player. Choose a score keeper to record each player's score. The player with the highest score after three turns is the winner (adapted from Virginia Beach, 1971).

- Give each set of partners a target such as: a bucket, plastic bottle, piece of tape on the wall. The two partners compete against each other for points. Encourage them to stand away from the target. Award two points for any successful throw from behind a 15-foot line. Any successful throw in front of this line earns one point.
- Divide the children into teams. A team scores one point each time it successfully hits the opposite team's target.

KEY POINTS:

→ Praise the skill and hard work it takes to complete the task. Encourage the child to select a target and persist until a good toss results.

# BAG PILE

MATERIALS:

beanbags

ACTIVITIES:

Set the children up in several equal lines. Place a pile of beanbags in front of each line. On a signal, the first player begins to pass the beanbags back one at a time. When the last player in each line receives the bags, he or she begins to stack them. The stack must stand by itself and no one is allowed to help the last player stack the beanbags. The first team with a standing stack of beanbags wins one point. The players all move back one space and the end player takes the beanbags up front and becomes the first player in the line. The game can be played to a certain number of points or until all players have had a turn to stack the beanbags. The team with the highest score wins (adapted from Virginia Beach, 1971).

- Ask each member of a team to run to a designated spot, pick a beanbag, take it back to the stack and stack it themselves.
- Give each team their choice—either stack all the beanbags on top of each other on a large surface (i.e. table, floor) or stack three less than the total number of beanbags on top of a cone or gallon plastic milk jug.

KEY POINTS:

Stress the point that the child's efforts and skill were responsible for the outcome of the task.

# MOUSETRAP

MATERIALS:

> record player
>
> records

ACTIVITIES:

Divide the children into two groups. One group finds partners and makes a trap anywhere in the playing area. The trap is made by the partners facing each other and holding hands above their shoulders. The other group begins walking under the traps when a signal is given by the parent.

When the parent says "Snap," the trap shuts to catch any player in the trap. Any player caught finds another player who was caught and forms a trap. The game continues until all players are caught (adapted from Duval, 1977-1978).

- Use music and allow the traps to shut when the music stops.
- Vary the types of movement (i.e. walk, jump, skip, etc.).

KEY POINTS:

→ Reinforce the ability to follow directions and the strategy necessary to "catch" a player.

# SNOWBALL

MATERIALS:

> bounceable balls
>
> yarn balls

ACTIVITIES:

Divide the children into two equal teams and give each team an equal number of balls (about five or six each). On signal, players attempt to hit opposing players with the balls. Any player who is hit must move to the sideline. Sidelined players may retrieve balls and throw them to teammates, but they may not throw them at opponents. The game ends when one player remains.

- Give each player a yarn ball and play as above.
- Do not eliminate players for being hit.
- The only hit that counts is if a person is hit on the foot.

KEY POINTS:

→ Reinforce the children for working together with teammates. Encourage the effort necessary to accurately throw and hit a teammate.

# CREATE YOUR OWN ACTIVITIES

MATERIALS NECESSARY:

EXAMPLES OF ACTIVITIES:

KEY POINTS TO BE EMPHASIZED:

# *ORGANIZED PLAY (6-8 YEAR OLDS)*

## BRITISH BULLDOG

MATERIALS:

```
ropes

tape
```

ACTIVITIES:

The children line up on one of the two boundary lines (use ropes or tape). Choose two players to stand in the center of the playing area. These two players are the "Bulldogs" and attempt to catch players running from one line to the other. On the signal "British Bulldog" all of the players try to run to the opposite line without getting caught.

The center players must try to catch a player running from one line to the other, raise that player's hand and shout "British Bulldog 1-2-3." Any player that is caught becomes a "Bulldog." The game continues until all players are caught.

- Use a variety of motor skills (i.e. run, jump, skip, etc.)
- Increase the number of "Bulldogs" and/or the space.

KEY POINTS:

→ Stress the importance of skill and effort at dodging and running.

# BARNYARD GOLF

MATERIALS:

> tin cans
>
> beanbags

ACTIVITIES:

Arrange numbered tin cans around the yard. Each child starts at a "hole" (tin can) and throws his or her beanbag to the next "hole" in the sequence. If the child gets the beanbag in the "hole," he or she gets one point. Each child then picks up his or her beanbag and attempts to throw it to the next "hole."

- Vary the distance between "holes."
- Set two different distances for each "hole" and allow a player to score one point from the closer mark and two points from the farther mark.
- Vary the type of throw to be used.
- Use one can for each child so that all are playing at the same time.
- Use a scoring system like golf; the lowest score is the best.

KEY POINTS:

→ Reinforce the ability to follow directions as well as the ability necessary to score a hole in-one.

# JUMP THE SHOT

MATERIALS:

```
ropes
```

ACTIVITIES:

One person holds a long rope and swings it in a circle keeping one end on the floor. The child jumps the rope as it comes around.

- When the child becomes successful at the farthest end of the rope, he or she moves closer to the person swinging the rope where the height of the rope above the ground is greater.
- If more than one participates, children hold hands and learn to jump with a partner.

KEY POINTS:

→ Reinforce the child's jumping skill and hard work.

# CATCHING A BALL

MATERIALS:

balls of various sizes

ACTIVITIES:

Child catches a ball properly by putting his or her body behind the ball and bending at the knees so as to "give" with the catch.

- Vary the size of the balls being caught.
- The child works toward catching an increasing number of balls in a row.
- Catch from different angles; catch balls thrown high to low.

KEY POINTS:

→ Praise the hard work and skill it takes to be a good catcher.

# KICKING A SOCCER BALL

MATERIALS:

```
soccer balls

or

playground balls
```

ACTIVITIES:

- Child keeps the ball under control within an area of 6 feet wide while running.
- Same as above, only the goal now is to complete the skill in less and less time (i.e. 1 minute, 45 seconds, 30 seconds, etc.).

KEY POINTS:

→ Encourage and reinforce the effort put forth in completing the task of keeping the soccer ball under control.

# PARTNER TOSS

MATERIALS:

balloons

water

ACTIVITIES:

- Play catch with a balloon filled with water.
- Each partner must toss the balloon gently.
- Start close together and then move farther apart.

KEY POINTS:

→ Compliment the child's effort and patience at completing the task. Praise the child for the effort expended in trying to catch the balloon.

## STAND UP

MATERIALS:

| |
|---|
| none |

ACTIVITIES:

- Children of similar size sit on the floor, back to back. They link arms at the elbows and by pushing backward, must be able to stand (without placing their hands on the floor).
- Children should learn to sit back down.

KEY POINTS:

→ Reinforce the effort and performing the skill according to the directions.

# WATERSLIDE

MATERIALS:

plastic tarp

garden hose

ACTIVITIES:

Spread a long plastic tarp on the ground. Cover it with water from a hose and watch your child run and slide down it.

- The child should try it on his or her stomach, back, seat, etc.
- Try it with a partner.

KEY POINTS:

→ Encourage the child to keep trying the task and then reinforce the persistence.

# CREATE YOUR OWN ACTIVITIES

MATERIALS NECESSARY:

EXAMPLES OF ACTIVITIES:

KEY POINTS:

→

# 5
# UNDERSTANDING GOAL SETTING

```
Key issues to be addressed in this chapter:

• Understanding Goal Setting
• Learning How to Set Goals
• Assisting in Setting Goals
• Reinforcing Goal Setting Behaviors
• Helping Children to Set Their Own Goals
```

## UNDERSTANDING GOAL SETTING

Your child must be helped to learn to set goals and work toward completing tasks. Following failure, it is especially important that your child understand that performance can be changed. Help him or her to understand that failure on the task was due in part to things which can be changed, such as not enough effort expended, or goals which were set too high.

When realistic goals are set, success can be expected. If the goals are too difficult, failure will often result. But who is to say what is a success and what is a failure? One person's concept of success may be very different from another's. Regardless, when individuals are successful in learning or doing something, they feel better about themselves. The level of success depends upon the standard of excellence which has been set.

The setting of standards is affected by personal goals or expectations which are compared to performance on a task. Personal feelings of success or failure are related to your degree of achievement motivation. This affects goals which are seen as important and the manner in which goals are set.

It is unrealistic to set high goals if you know the goals cannot be reached. Realistic goals must be set to prevent automatic failure situations. Parents can help the low achiever who always fails by helping him or her set more realistic goals. The media, teachers, friends, etc. tell children, even at an early age, what it means to be successful. It is the parent's responsibility to help each child set realistic goals and definitions of success.

# LEARNING HOW TO SET GOALS

In order to help your child learn to set goals, you must:
- ► Determine your child's present ability.
- ► Consider the next logical step.
- ► Help your child state a new goal in measurable terms (time or quantity).
- ► Set a time line for your child to use to meet the new goal.
- ► Provide a way to evaluate (and praise) the accomplishment of the goal.
- ► Help your child reset the goal to the next step.

112

An example of this process may help. Let us assume we wish to help a child learn to control a hammer and nail.

| Step | Hammering |
|---|---|
| • Present level | Can hammer 3 pieces of wood together |
| • Determine the next logical step | Four pieces of wood should be nailed together to form a model. |
| • Help child set new goals | Pat says, "I would like to build a ship out of four pieces of wood." |
| • Set time line | Parents say, "When will you build your ship?" Pat says, "By 10:00 today. Then I will paint it tomorrow." |
| • Measure outcome | At 10:00, check to see if Pat has finished the ship. If not, help the process. If so, praise Pat and help her go to a new task or set a new goal. |

# ASSISTING IN SETTING GOALS

The goal setting cycle begins with the parent providing standards of excellence about a task and helping the child set a realistic goal to be attained. As the child engages in the task, the parent praises acceptable behaviors by showing warmth. With improved performance, parents should grant greater independence.

Parents can help their children learn to work toward desirable goals by structuring their play environment. If a sequence of more and more difficult tasks can be identified, children can be encouraged to master each step. For example, most children love to build with blocks. This play activity can be easily used to help children learn the value of setting goals, and achieving them one step at a time.

As parents, you can help your children state or set goals for themselves. When you set challenges or goals, attempt to present them in positive, measurable terms.

| **Vague Goals** | → **Specific Goals** |
|---|---|
| • Learn to jump better. | Jump 5 times in a row without stopping. |
| • Be able to jump rope. | Jump rope 10 times without missing. |
| • Build a block house. | Build a block house 3 stories tall. |

Goals and expectations are individual, and should be both realistic and specific. Your child must be allowed to help set his or her own goals. If realistic goals are set, success will occur more often. In some situations failure may still occur. When this happens, it is important for the child to understand what caused the failure, and what might be done to produce a success in the future.

For success, your child needs:

► Challenges and Appropriate Goals
► Responsibility
► Feedback
► Support and Encouragement

Parents have the chance to create situations that invite their child to discover and explore new ways to perform tasks. Children should be encouraged to do their best, whatever the task. Use praise for those efforts when efforts are good. Children should be encouraged to stretch their abilities. Play activities which have measurable outcomes are particularly helpful. For example, you may wish to ask your child:

► How many blocks can you use to build a house?
► Can you use four colors in your picture?
► How many beads can you string?
► How many ingredients can you use to bake today?
► How many pieces of railroad track can you link together?

Activities such as these help your child see improvement each and every day.

There are many types of play activities that can be used to help the child measure abilities. Activities such as stacking building blocks, playing with objects such as balls, and learning to cook or sew can all be challenges for a child.

# REINFORCING GOAL SETTING BEHAVIORS

It is wise to provide positive reinforcement when your child is successful in an attempt to reach a goal. A smile or pat on the back does wonders to show that you approve.

By using positive comments, you can provide positive reinforcement to make sure that a task or challenge is repeated. Reinforcement includes the verbal encouragement that is given, such as "Nice try, you really used your legs to jump that time," or "I bet if you take your time and straighten out those ropes or boxes, it will be easier to climb." In this case the reinforcement is positive and helpful.

Accomplishments should be rewarded, but attention and praise should also be given for hard work and effort. Even if the expected goal is not reached, let your child know that the effort was important. By praising effort, parents are saying the process is important in reaching the goal. Often, parents only praise the goal when it is achieved and do not praise the means for reaching the goal.

By giving directions in a positive manner and providing positive reinforcement, parents help their child to be successful. Children need large
amounts of success so it will not be unbearable when they meet failure. If
children do not have a wide range of success then they will be so afraid of
making mistakes that difficult tasks will be avoided. When too few suc-
cesses have been encountered, an unsuccessful experience may become too
important to the child. Encouragement should be provided so children
understand that mistakes are not the end of the world. Goal setting
behaviors and the efforts that may lead to success must be reinforced.

Parents can offer suggestions and give directions in a positive manner. By
showing their child *how* to do a task and how to be successful, parents are
aiding in solving a problem or completing a task. The goal-setting techniques discussed in this chapter are a convenient way to assist your child in
becoming successful.

Praise has a very strong influence on your child's behavior. Everyone
responds to the nice things people say and do by repeating whatever action
caused the reinforcement. When someone says, "Thank you" for opening
the door, or "Nice try, I'm proud of you," you are more likely to try again
in the future. As parents it is important to recognize the value of these comments and to use them to reinforce desired behaviors in your child.

It is important to realize that praise and rewards must be used carefully or your child will become completely dependent upon them. The ultimate goal is to help your child learn to value hard work and complete tasks for their own sake. This will help your child in becoming self-motivated. This self-motivation is best attained by initially praising the desired behaviors and then by talking with your child about how good it felt to accomplish the act. This sense of "feeling good" will become a reward in itself and you will no longer have to be constantly present to give out rewards of affection and approval.

Parents should encourage and help their children set goals which are challenging but not too difficult by (1) *offering general encouragement* as well as instruction and giving approval when a difficult task is accomplished, (2) learning to distinguish between "pushing" and "pulling," and learning to *pull children from in front* by setting a good example, and (3) *emphasizing desirable goals*. This strategy is better than forcing children to attempt tasks or constantly comparing them to other children. An important factor, however, is to display interest and involvement in your child's activities.

Parents communicate positive attitudes toward their child in many verbal as well as non-verbal ways. For example, the following behaviors are generally perceived as reinforcements which contribute to the development of positive self-concepts:

- smile
- wink
- joking with them
- praising them in front of others
- playing or practicing *with* them

- pat on the back
- thumbs up sign
- arm on shoulder
- V for Victory sign
- O.K. sign

In addition, your child will feel good when he or she believes you genuinely care. For example, helping to readjust goals, planning new practice techniques or game strategies, and asking his or her advice all indicate that you value your child as an individual.

These positive techniques are particularly important after an individual feels he or she has performed or behaved poorly. It is critical that your child feels important and accepted even if performance was bad on a particular occasion. Acceptance as an individual must never be dependent upon good performance.

# HELPING THE CHILD TO SET GOALS

Children must learn to judge their present skill level. For example, ask your child:

"How many blocks can you stack in a tower?"

"Can you jump over a rope held this high (6 inches)?"

"Can you bounce a ball four times in a row?"

Use this information to help shape the next level of challenge. For example, if a three-year-old can stack four blocks, ask about stacking five. Tommie, a five-year-old, can jump over a rope as high as his ankle. Ask him to jump twice that high by next week. Susie, a six-year-old, can toss and catch a ball four times in a row. Challenge her to do it five times in a row.

Notice that each challenge is related to the child's own ability. Children must learn to value their own skills and work toward improving these skills and abilities. Goals should seldom be set in a comparative fashion. To catch the ball five times in a row is very important. But for a child to say, "I will catch it more times than Jane" is not a personal achievement statement. We can always find "someone else to be better than," but children must learn to do better themselves every day.

The purpose of playing games is to provide interaction between the child and the game. Therefore, if the parent is to use games effectively as a learning medium then it must be understood how to make use of games to enhance achievement motivation. For example, instead of setting the final goal as winning or losing, you can help your child to achieve success by establishing shorter goals at various levels (progressive goals).

When the number of rules is increased, more strategy required, or additional players included, the parent must be aware of resetting the goals. When the goals are reset, then the child must take greater risks, not just physical risks, but risks of failure and opportunities for success. Therefore, the child becomes more goal-oriented.

With higher goals, your child knows what he or she must work toward. At this point you must be aware of providing knowledge of results; that is, information to the child about performance. With increased knowledge about the performance, your child is increasing his or her motive to achieve. In this instance, you are allowing your child to take responsibility for his or her actions. You do not want your child to blame himself or herself, but to know how to perform better in the future.

As you observe the play of your child notice if the activity will help develop the important aspects of achievement motivation. For example, does the activity:

► have measurable goals?
► allow your child to measure his or her progress?
► encourage personal initiative?
► value independence?
► allow your child to control his or her efforts?
► provide well-defined responsibilities or roles?
► encourage new challenges?

By using the format of the Model Program the tasks can be written down and the child can check off his or her achievement and progress on a task. This record can provide feedback for you, as well as your child.

In conclusion, permitting your child to learn to do tasks on his or her own will achieve several objectives.

► Your child will develop more responsibility, for individual performance will be developed.
► Individualized learning will begin to develop.
► Independence will begin to develop.
► Self-direction will be learned and performance controlled in small steps.

The following information will provide you with some sample activities for your child. Take time to use one or more activities with your child, or modify your own activities.

# MODEL PROGRAM

Activity: *Block Building*

|  | LEVEL 1 | LEVEL 2 | LEVEL 3 |
|---|---|---|---|
| TASK No. 1 | ◯<br>Given 2 blocks stack 1 beside the other | ◯<br>Given 3 blocks stack 1 beside the others | ◯<br>Given 4 blocks stack 1 beside the others |
| TASK No. 2 | ◯<br>Given 2 blocks stack 1 on top of the other | ◯<br>Given 3 blocks stack 1 on top of the others | ◯<br>Given 4 blocks stack 1 on top of of the others |
| TASK No. 3 | ◯<br>Given 3 blocks stack 1 on top of 2 | ◯<br>Given 5 blocks stack 2 blocks on top of 3 | ◯<br>Given 7 blocks stack 3 blocks on top of 4 |
| TASK No. 4 | ◯<br>Given 6 blocks stack 1 on top of 2 on top of 3 | ◯<br>Given 10 blocks stack 1 on top of 2 on top of 3 on top of 4 | ◯<br>Given 15 blocks stack 1 on top of 2 on top of 3 on top of 4 on top of 5 |

Changes in the qualitative demands of a play activity create a whole range of tasks to be completed. Parents should remember that changing the task supports the following beliefs:

► Breaking down a task into simple parts promotes easier learning.
► Interest and motivation will increase because each child can be successful.

The form on the following page will assist you in setting up tasks for your child. Follow the Model Program to help in beginning this process.

# PARENT-CHILD WORKSHEET

Activity: _____

Indicate in the circle when the task at each level is completed.

|  | LEVEL 1 | LEVEL 2 |
|---|---|---|
| TASK 1 | String 4 beads in a row, with no 2 beads of the same color side by side. ○ | ○ |
| TASK 2 | ○ | ○ |
| TASK 3 | ○ | ○ |
| TASK 4 | ○ | ○ |

# WORKSHEET

**Set Daily Tasks**

Using the model program as a guide, let your child attempt to set his or her own goals for a task of your own choosing. Let the child work on his or her own, using you as a guide. Encourage your child to put forth his or her best effort. This activity can be done either on a daily (one task per day) or weekly (one task to be worked on for the week) basis.

Activity: _____

|  | Level 1 | Level 2 |
|---|---|---|
| Day or Task 1: | | |
| Day or Task 2: | | |
| Day or Task 3: | | |
| Day or Task 4: | | |
| Day or Task 5: | | |

# KEY CONCEPTS

- Help your child learn to set goals.
- Show support and encouragement.
- Help your child to measure his or her progress.
- Encourage new challenges.

## Suggested Readings

Cahoon, O. W., Price, A. H., Scoresby, K. L. *Parents and the achieving child.* Provo, Utah: Brigham Young University Press, 1979.

Bentley, W. G. *Learning to move and moving to learn.* New York: Citation Press, 1970.

# GOAL SETTING ACTIVITIES

## *FINE MOTOR (3-5 YEAR OLDS)*

### TAKE APART AND PUT TOGETHER ACTIVITIES

MATERIALS:

> tinker toys
>
> toys to take apart
>
> nesting boxes
>
> coffee cans (various sizes) with lids
>
> washers, nuts, bolts
>
> wooden puzzles
>
> pegs and pegboard

ACTIVITIES:

- Put all the boxes inside one box; all lids on the cans; all pegs in the pegboard; etc.
- Make a sun with the pegs in the pegboard; a house; a car; etc.
- Put all red pegs at the top of the pegboard; blue pegs at the bottom; etc.
- Make a building out of 5 different things.
- Connect 2 pieces of wood together with nuts, bolts and washers; 3 pieces; 5 pieces; etc.

KEY POINTS:

→ Stress setting a goal that has a measurable outcome. When the child can meet his or her first goal, encourage the setting of a new goal.

# BUILDING ACTIVITIES

MATERIALS:

blocks

scrap wood, hammer, nails

tubes

Playskool blocks

tin cans

nuts, bolts, washers pieces of wood (holes drilled)

ACTIVITIES:

- Stack 3 blocks; 5 blocks; 7 blocks; etc.
- Make an airplane with 2 pieces of wood; a birdhouse with 4 pieces.
- Make the cans stretch as far as they can; reach as high as they can; etc.
- Make a house or train with three levels.

KEY POINTS:

→ Observe the child's present accomplishment and help him or her progress to the next logical step.

# MANIPULATIVE ACTIVITIES

MATERIALS:

boxes

buckets

cans

small blocks, stones

pots, pans, cooking utensils

empty food containers

wooden cubes

dominoes

buttons, marbles, beads

ACTIVITIES:

- Put the stones in the can with both hands; 1 hand; the other hand; 2 fingers; etc.
- Put the wooden cubes in the container one at a time.
- Stack the dominoes in a tall stack.
- Put all the right lids on the pots and containers.
- String all the buttons and beads.

KEY POINTS:

→ Emphasize setting a realistic goal and working toward it.

# ARTS AND CRAFTS ACTIVITIES

MATERIALS:

> pipe cleaners
>
> paper bags
>
> Playdoh
>
> clay

ACTIVITIES:

- Make an animal with 2 pipe cleaners (3, 4, 5) or clay.
- Make a mask with the paper bag; a hat.
- Make cookies with the Playdoh. Cook the cookies; serve them to company.
- Shape the clay into a ball; square; triangle; etc.

KEY POINTS:

→ Reinforce the effort it takes to reach the desired goal. Stress setting the goal and then working to accomplish it.

# CREATE YOUR OWN ACTIVITIES

MATERIALS NECESSARY:

EXAMPLES OF ACTIVITIES:

KEY POINTS TO BE EMPHASIZED:

# *FINE MOTOR (6-8 YEAR OLDS)*

## CUT-OUT ACTIVITIES

MATERIALS:

> geometric forms
>
> paper
>
> scissors
>
> pencils, crayons

ACTIVITIES:

- Trace around the circle form and color; square; etc.
- Trace around the form and cut it out.
- Put several of the cut-out forms together to form a picture.
- Trace around the form and color everything outside the figures.

KEY POINTS:

→ Reinforce selecting a goal that is the next logical step beyond the child's present ability level.

# SEWING ACTIVITIES

MATERIALS:

```
sewing cards

string

yarn
```

ACTIVITIES:

- Sew the numbers on the card, such as one to two, two to three, etc.
- Sew the design on the card, such as a circle; triangle; square, etc.
- Make a design of your own.
- Write your name with yarn on the sewing card.

KEY POINTS:

→ Reinforce selecting a task and reaching the pre-set goal.

# SEQUENCING ACTIVITIES

MATERIALS:

> colored beads
>
> string
>
> card patterns

ACTIVITIES:

- String the beads at random.
- String 10 beads as fast as possible.
- String according to a color named (i.e. red, blue).
- String according to card patterns (refer to Chapter 6).

KEY POINTS:

→ Stress the skill and effort necessary to reach the goal.

# MARBLE ACTIVITIES

MATERIALS:

marbles

tennis ball

golf ball

ACTIVITIES:

With one of the marbles:

- aim and shoot at a tennis ball.
- aim and shoot at a golf ball.
- aim and shoot at another marble.
- try to shoot another marble out of the ring.
- attempt to hit 5 of 10 marbles.
- hit all the blue marbles.

KEY POINTS:

→ Emphasize setting a goal that has an observable outcome.

# CREATIVE ACTIVITIES

MATERIALS:

```
toothpicks

paper
```

ACTIVITIES:

- Make a circle on a flat surface; square; triangle; etc.
- Write your name; the alphabet; etc.
- Outline a house; make a smaller house to fit in the big house.
- Make a box as high as possible.
- Can you make a circle, etc.?

KEY POINTS:

→ Observe the child's present ability and proceed to the next step.

# MANIPULATIVE ACTIVITIES

MATERIALS:

rocks of all sizes

paper cups

ACTIVITIES:

- Put rocks into the cup with the right hand; left hand; switching hands.
- Only use 2 fingers to put the rocks into the cup; left hand; right hand; switch.
- Put rocks into the cup as quickly as possible with right hand; left hand; switch.

KEY POINTS:

→ Allow the child to see the increasing difficulty in the task. Let the children time themselves.

# CREATE YOUR OWN ACTIVITIES

MATERIALS NECESSARY:

EXAMPLES OF ACTIVITIES:

KEY POINTS TO BE EMPHASIZED:

→

# *UNSTRUCTURED PLAY (3-8 YEAR OLDS)*

In unstructured play the child is initiating the activity. You are helping to guide your child toward goal setting expectations.

## JUMPING ACTIVITIES

MATERIALS:

```
inner tubes

old mattress

ropes

low boxes

wagon

scooters
```

If your child is engaging in these activities, then encourage:

- jumping on the inner tube 5 times; 10 times; 15 times; etc.
- pretending the wagon is a sport car; a pick-up; a fire truck; etc.
- jumping on and over the box 2 times; 3 times; 4 times; etc.
- jumping over the rope while held at a low level; raise the rope a few inches and jump; raise again; etc.

KEY POINTS:

→ Encourage the child to increase the goal with each successive attempt. Stress looking at present ability and progressing to the next, more difficult step.

# BLOCK ACTIVITIES

MATERIALS:

blocks

cans

boxes

If your child is playing with blocks, then:

- encourage child to build a block tower or other structure
- observe the height or shape of the tower and ask if another one a little taller can be built; can the height be increased; can the child make a different shape?

KEY POINTS:

→ Observe the present ability and help the child strive for another step.

# COOKING ACTIVITIES

MATERIALS:

```
spoons

pots

pans

cans
```

If your child is playing with cooking utensils, then:

- let the child choose a recipe with four ingredients

- encourage their cooking so that tomorrow they can choose a recipe with five ingredients.

KEY POINTS:

→ Help the child see that each time he or she bakes, he or she is accomplishing a more difficult task.

# PROP BOX ACTIVITIES

MATERIALS:

Grocery Store Box:

pictures of workers, play money, cash register, paper bags

Carpenter's Box:

pictures of carpenters at work and tools, equipment, ruler, some toy tools, empty can, brushes

Plumber's Box:

pictures of plumbers at work and tools, wrench, faucets, pipe and fittings

Post Office Box:

picture of mailcarrier at work, old shoulder bag, envelopes, stamps or seals, rubber stamps

Doctor's Box:

pictures of doctors and nurses at work, bandages, pill bottles, gauze, tape, small purse or box for doctor's bag

Fire Station Box:

pictures of fire station, trucks and workers, fire hat, rubber raincoat, pair of boots

Shoe Store Box:

pictures of shoes, people having feet measured and trying on shoes, ruler, shoe boxes, shoe horn

If your child is engaged in these activities, then encourage:

- being a grocery clerk.
- being a carpenter fixing a broken chair.
- being a plumber fixing a leaky faucet.
- being a doctor when someone has a bad cold.

KEY POINTS:

→ Reinforce the carrying out of tasks through to an end goal.

# PRETEND ACTIVITIES

MATERIALS:

| | |
|---|---|
| toy animals | play money |
| dollhouse furniture, people | plastic plants, watering can |
| dress-up clothes | small step ladder |
| table and chairs | baby rattles, bottles, clothes, diapers |
| broom and dustpan | |
| telephone | puppets |
| | rhythm instruments |
| mirror | |

If your child is engaged in these activities, then encourage:

- calling the grocery store for groceries.
- being a mother or father feeding the baby.
- being a zoo keeper and feeding your toy animals.
- setting the table for dinner.

KEY POINTS:

→ Stress setting a goal and reaching it.

# PUZZLE ACTIVITIES

MATERIALS:

```
pictures

puzzles

shapes
```

If your child is playing with puzzles, then:

- have a variety of puzzles available. Be sure that they vary in size of pieces and complexity. Help the child begin with an easy one and gradually choose more difficult ones.
- have 3-4 different puzzles.
- help children create puzzles out of pictures.
- vary difficulty by changing the puzzle piece, size, shape or colors.

KEY POINTS:

→ Stress the importance of having progressively more difficult puzzles, with an end result that can be measured by you and/or your child.

# CREATE YOUR OWN ACTIVITIES

MATERIALS NECESSARY:

EXAMPLES OF ACTIVITIES:

KEY POINTS TO BE EMPHASIZED:

# ORGANIZED PLAY (3-5 YEAR OLDS)

## BEANBAG TOSS

MATERIALS:

```
beanbags

targets
```

ACTIVITIES:

- Child throws a beanbag into a container using an underhand toss. The container can be a box with a clown's face painted on it, garbage can or anything else.
- Increase the distance between the child and the container (such as from 2 feet, to 3 feet, 4 feet, etc.).
- Predict how many will land in the target (2 of 5; 3 of 5; 4 of 5; etc.).

KEY POINTS:

→ Emphasize setting a realistic goal and striving for it.

# ROLL THE BALL

MATERIALS:

balls of various sizes

ACTIVITIES:

Parent and children sit on the floor in a circle. The parent rolls the ball to a child after having said, for example, "I'll roll the ball to..." The child stops the ball with both hands and rolls it to another child after having said, "I'll roll the ball to..."

- Increase the distance between the children as they become more successful in rolling and stopping the ball (i.e. a distance of 2 feet; increase it to 3 feet; 4 feet; etc.).
- Use balls of various sizes. The smaller the ball, the more difficult the game will be (i.e. an 8″ playground ball, 6″ playground ball, tennis ball, golf ball, etc.).
- Decrease the amount of time the child can hold the ball as in "Hot Potato" (i.e. 10 seconds, 8 seconds, 6 seconds, etc.).

KEY POINTS:

→ Emphasize setting goals that have measurable outcomes.

# RING TOSS

**MATERIALS:**

> rubber rings
>
> targets
>
> stakes
>
> hoops

**ACTIVITIES:**

- Toss rings at target (Score: 2 points for ringers, 1 point if it lands on base).
- The level of challenge may be changed by simply moving the throwing line (from 2 feet to 3 feet, 4 feet, etc.).
- If there is more than one player, give each child a set of rings and drive a stake in the ground for a target for each child. All players can participate simultaneously and a partner can record the scores. Predict how many points will be scored.

**KEY POINTS:**

→ Emphasize setting a realistic goal.

# BOUNCE A BALL

MATERIALS:

> various bounceable
> balls

ACTIVITIES:

Child uses two hands to bounce a ball. Provide a ball for each child in the activity.

- Specify a number of bounces that must be successfully completed in a row (i.e. 3, 5, 7, etc.).
- Vary the size of the balls to be bounced. (Use progressively smaller balls.)
- Use right hand, left hand and alternate hands for specific number of bounces (i.e. 3, 5, 7, etc.)
- Walk a given distance while bouncing the ball, increasing either the distance (such as 10 feet, 15 feet, etc.) or number of bounces (such as 4 bounces, 5, 6, 7, etc.).

KEY POINTS:

→ Stress looking at present ability level and realistically determining the next logical step.

# OBSTACLE COURSE

MATERIALS:

obstacles

boxes

cones

chairs

tires

ACTIVITIES:

- Start out with 3 pieces in the obstacle course, then add 1 more, 2 more, 3 more pieces.
- Change movement pattern from walking to running, crawling, etc. between the objects.
- Decrease the amount of time to complete the course.

KEY POINTS:

→ Emphasize the increasing difficulty of the task.

# CREATE YOUR OWN ACTIVITIES

MATERIALS NECESSARY:

EXAMPLES OF ACTIVITIES:

KEY POINTS TO BE EMPHASIZED:

→

# *ORGANIZED PLAY (6-8 YEAR OLDS)*

## BALL TOSS

MATERIALS:

balls of
various sizes

shapes

ACTIVITIES:

- Toss ball while stepping forward on opposite foot (underhand, overhand).
- Same as above, only toss the ball at a target (such as a garbage can, hoop, etc.).
- Begin with a large target and decrease its size as the child is successful in hitting it (such as 1 hit, 2 hits, 3, 4, etc.).
- Specify a particular number of tosses to hit the target (such as 1, 2, 3, etc.).
- Increase the number as the child is successful in tossing the specified number (number of hits plus one more, 2 more, etc.).

KEY POINTS:

→ Stress setting a goal that can be reached and then increasing it.

# HOP IN TIRE OR HOOPS

MATERIALS:

---

hoops

inner tubes

tires

---

ACTIVITIES:

- Run through the scattered hoops.
- Increase the number of hoops, tires, or circles in which the child must hop (such as 3 hoops, 4, 5, 6, 7, etc.).
- Hop backward rather than forward into a given number of circles (such as 3, 4, 5, 6, etc.).

KEY POINTS:

→ Emphasize setting goals that have measurable outcomes.

# ROLL AT TARGET

MATERIALS:

> balls
>
> Indian clubs
>
> empty milk cartons
>
> targets

ACTIVITIES:

- Take five turns at rolling a ball at an Indian club, milk carton or plastic container. One point is given each time the child hits the target.
- Increase the distance between the bowler and the club as bowler becomes successful in turning over the club (such as 3 feet, 5 feet, 7 feet, 9 feet, etc.).
- Use balls of various sizes (such as basketball, softball, tennis ball, golf ball).

KEY POINTS:

→ Stress determining the next logical step from present ability level.

# CREATE YOUR OWN ACTIVITIES

MATERIALS NECESSARY:

EXAMPLES OF ACTIVITIES:

KEY POINTS TO BE EMPHASIZED:

→

# 6
# UNDERSTANDING THE IMPORTANCE OF INDEPENDENCE

Key issues to be addressed in this chapter:
- Understanding the Importance of Independence
- Becoming Aware of Your Role as a Parent
- Actively Involving Children
- Reinforcing Independent Behavior

Play is a powerful way for your child to be the master of his or her environment. If the imaginary play of children is watched, it can be noticed how the "good guy" usually wins. Children are able to conquer problems in the environment and/or reverse the circumstances of the play. "Make believe" play is a positive way for children to express themselves and to begin to develop positive images related to their ability.

It is critical that an atmosphere of freedom and encouragement be established. Your personal attitudes will determine the amount of freedom and responsibility fostered in your child.

The young child who is confined and overprotected will not grow into an independent, self-reliant adult. However, it is important not to confuse independence training with total permissiveness. Children must discover that there are boundaries and limits to behavior. The child must learn to accept the responsibility for making choices and also for accepting the choices, rules and authority of others.

# BECOMING AWARE OF YOUR ROLE AS A PARENT

Parents must begin to allow children to be independent as their skills and abilities develop. Children's attitudes are influenced by the information they get from others about their achievement efforts. Some parents may provide too little independence, too much over-protection, and not enough problem-solving activities. These parental behaviors may result in lower self-confidence, lower goals, dependence on others, and a higher need to be loved and protected.

Children need to have the freedom to explore and parents should encourage this exploration. In the early years, children use play to learn about the world. Play allows for social interaction with others and for free expression of thoughts, ideas and feelings. Parents should encourage children's play and play with them whenever possible. It is not necessary to play every minute of the day, but it is important to make the time spent playing with children *quality* time. Enjoy your child's activities whether it is talking on a play telephone or playing "Hide-and-Go-Seek." By playing with you, your child learns about his or her surroundings and receives important cues as to acceptance into the world.

What a parent expects may dictate what type of play a child demonstrates. Parents influence their children's choices for toy preference or certain play behaviors by indicating the sex appropriateness or inappropriateness of the activity or toy. This type of influencing may prevent some children, especially girls, from enjoying the satisfaction of independent accomplishments. Unfortunately, such biasing may limit the child's choices and the experiences available to that child. Children need to be free to explore and discover and should not be hindered by the adult-imposed ideas about appropriate activities or objects.

Children should be encouraged to role play and "try on" various adult roles. Girls must not only play nurse but play doctor, too. Boys should play the dancer as well as the football star. All children should be encouraged to experiment with different roles and activities.

Parents who expect their children to be independent and to do well at an early age tend to have children who wish to do well and who work hard to learn and grow. That is, parents who expect and require self-reliance early in life and who allow their children freedom to explore around the house, backyard, and neighborhood will help their children learn to value hard work and its rewards. Mothers and fathers who reward self-reliant behavior with affection and also insist on responsibility develop children who desire to do well.

Wise parents and others who care must attempt to provide experiences which allow their children to accept and meet challenges head on. These activities will also help in developing the ability to set realistic expectations. But sometimes as they learn to become self-sufficient and independent, their attempts and efforts at solving problems must be reinforced to a greater extent than their actual accomplishments. It is the process, or the desire to learn and attempt challenges, that is much more important than the results of their efforts.

# ACTIVELY INVOLVING CHILDREN

Your child should be taught to (a) take responsibility for his or her own efforts and abilities, (b) take an active part in making decisions, and (c) take responsibility for success or failure on a task. Children should learn to control their own play activities. It is important for both boys and girls to be able to determine their own level of involvement and to have control over the outcome of their play.

# REINFORCING INDEPENDENT BEHAVIOR

It is important that you show positive reactions to your child's activities. That is not to say that you must let them have the run of the house, but it is important that you encourage their creativity and desire to explore and understand everything. Let them know that you approve of banging things and learning to build. Perhaps even challenge them by giving them some new objects to master. These types of actions are important to children because they say, "You're O.K.!"

The way in which you relate to your children often provides information about what you value. For example, consider the way in which you make choices about your children. Whom do you ask to accept responsibility or demonstrate their competence? Take a moment to answer the questions in the "Parent Inventory."

# PARENT INVENTORY

| Whom do I ask to: | Son | Daughter | Either |
|---|---|---|---|
| set the table? | _____ | _____ | _____ |
| sweep the floor? | _____ | _____ | _____ |
| clean their rooms? | _____ | _____ | _____ |
| put their toys away? | _____ | _____ | _____ |
| dust? | _____ | _____ | _____ |
| dump the trash? | _____ | _____ | _____ |
| water the plants? | _____ | _____ | _____ |
| rake leaves? | _____ | _____ | _____ |
| take care of the family pet (dog, cat, etc.)? | _____ | _____ | _____ |
| be your helper? | _____ | _____ | _____ |

Consider your responses in the "Parent Inventory." Are there logical reasons why one child or group of children (e.g. boys vs. girls) is asked to do particular tasks? The household tasks identified by most parents do not seem to be particularly unique to one group of children. If your responses show a bias toward one child or another, can you make more equitable decisions?

The world of children should be filled with challenges to discover "Who am I?" and "What can I do?" Children need a large number of experiences in which they must cooperate with others in order to determine who they are, under what "rules" they operate, the limits to their freedom, and what is real. They are sensitive to their own personal identity. This awareness is especially noticeable as language becomes more important. The common statements of "I can do it!"..."Please let me try!"...or "I'm not a baby!" are open expressions that they are exploring their own competence. On the other hand, this same child may assert a need for protection and dependency as he or she resists challenges with statements such as "I can't do that, I'm just a baby!"

Boys and girls who are encouraged to solve their own problems grow to be self-reliant young men and women. They should be encouraged to identify their own goals and learn to work toward them. Children should learn to plot a course toward a specific accomplishment whether it be baking a pie, building a pyramid or bouncing a ball ten times in a row.

Observe your child's behavior in each of the play activities on pages 161-181. Note whether your child will stay with a task, or resume a challenge even if immediate success is not produced. These tasks will give you some indication about whether your child will stick with a difficult task. Help him or her learn the value of persistence, and sticking to a job, even if it is a difficult activity. If mistakes are made, assist your child in setting goals to overcome the problems.

Encourage your child to persist at challenging tasks. Set appropriate goals to assist the child in sticking to a task and succeeding. A child who does not choose challenging tasks or chooses tasks at which he or she has easily succeeded is showing characteristics of a low achiever. Try to encourage the child to choose more realistic and challenging tasks, and help him or her set new goals.

## OBSERVE YOUR CHILD

As you think about your child, answer the following questions regarding his or her play. Be prepared to discuss these behaviors with the teacher and identify ways to continue to develop the most positive aspects.

Does _____
　　　　　(your child's name)

|  | Yes | No |
|---|---|---|
| play in activities that have measurable goals? | _____ | _____ |
| show personal initiative? | _____ | _____ |
| show independence? | _____ | _____ |
| cooperate with others? | _____ | _____ |
| plan ahead or plot strategy? | _____ | _____ |
| actively involve himself or herself in the activity? | _____ | _____ |

# KEY CONCEPTS

- Independence and self-reliance are important.
- Provide opportunities to explore.
- Reinforce independence, self-reliance, and risk-taking.

## Suggested Readings

Dodson, J. Independence and your child. *Harpers Bazaar,* December, 1978, p. 161.
Fontana, V.J. Independence and the tie that binds. *Parents,* November, 1979, p. 88.
Weissbound, B. I do it myself (children). *Parents,* January, 1981, p. 84.
Weissbound, B. Struggle for independence. *Parents,* December, 1979, p. 76.

# RISK-TAKING ACTIVITIES

## *FINE MOTOR (3-8 YEAR OLDS)*

The activities that follow are examples of risk-taking activities for 3-8 year olds. These tasks encourage children to take the psychological risk of pursuing an increasingly difficult task. Some children tend to select tasks which are too easy or allow them to stay at their present ability level. They must be encouraged to strive to do better and better; to be willing to risk failing, and be willing to try again in order to be successful.

### Evaluation of Risk-Taking

Observe your child's behavior in each of the play activities. Note whether your child will stay with a task, or resume a challenge even if immediate success is not produced. These tasks will give you some indication about whether your child will stick with a difficult task. Help him or her learn the value of persistence, and sticking to a job, even if it is a difficult activity. If your child learns to risk failure, and learns that it is only through trying new things that real growth occurs, a lifelong love of learning will emerge.

# TASK 1

MATERIALS:

> beads of various
> colors to string
>
> cards with bead
> designs (variation:
> beads previously
> strung by the teacher)

ACTIVITIES:

Ask the child to reproduce each design correctly from memory. When two trials are failed, place before the child the first design, the last success, the first failure and the second failure. Instructions to the child are:

> "You may try one of these. Remember, this one was easy for you; this was not so easy but you got it right; this one was hard for you; and this one was very hard for you. Now which one would you like to try again?"

Allow the child a chance to resume the task. Refer to the section on "Evaluation of Risk Taking" to evaluate the child's performance.

Give the child the following bead designs on cards:

> red-blue-red-blue-red
> red-blue-blue-red-blue
> blue-red-red-red-red
> blue-red-blue-red-blue
> blue-blue-blue-red-blue

# TASK 2

MATERIALS:

> card with stick
> figures (as shown
> below)

ACTIVITIES:

Give the child the following "stick figure designs" on cards (modified from the Purdue Perceptual Motor Survey).

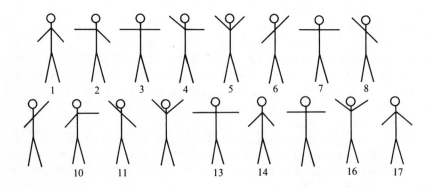

Ask the child to reproduce each design correctly from memory. When two trials are failed, place before the child the first design, the last success, the first failure and the second failure. Instructions to the child are:

> "You may try one of these. Remember, this one was easy for you; this was not so easy but you got it right; this one was hard for you; and this one was very hard for you. Now, which one would you like to try again?"

Allow the child a chance to resume the task. Refer to the section on "Evaluation of Risk Taking" to evaluate the child's performance.

# TASK 3

MATERIALS:

> blocks
>
> block designs on cards (as shown below)

ACTIVITIES:

Give the child the following block designs on cards.

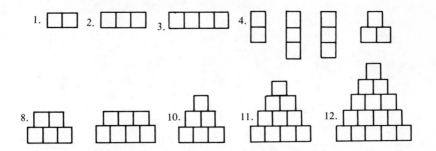

Ask the child to reproduce each design correctly from memory. When two trials are failed, place before the child the first design, the last success, the first failure and the second failure. Instructions to the child are:

> "You may try one of these. Remember, this one was easy for you; this was not so easy but you got it right; this one was hard for you; and this one was very hard for you. Now, which one would you like to try again?"

Allow the child a chance to resume the task. Refer to the section on "Evaluation of Risk Taking" to evaluate the child's performance.

# TASK 4

MATERIALS:

cards with pictures
(as shown below)

ACTIVITIES:

Show the child the following series of pictures mounted on construction paper (modified from Hagen Test of Selective Attention, 1978).

Ask the child to reproduce each design correctly from memory. When two trials are failed, place before the child the first design, the last success, the first failure and the second failure. Instructions to the child are:

> "You may try one of these. Remember, this one was easy for you; this was not so easy but you got it right; this one was hard for you; and this one was very hard for you. Now, which one would you like to try again?"

Allow the child a chance to resume the task. Refer to the section on "Evaluation of Risk Taking" to evaluate the child's performance.

# TASK 5

MATERIALS:

small red ball

plastic pail

marking tape

ACTIVITIES:

Give the child a small red ball to throw in a plastic pail from varying distances marked with tape. For example:
- 2 feet
- 3 feet
- 4 feet
- 5 feet

KEY POINTS:

→ Encourage your child to persist at challenging or difficult tasks. A child who does not choose challenging tasks or chooses tasks at which he or she has easily succeeded is showing characteristics of a low achiever. Try to encourage the child to choose more challenging tasks where the risk of failure is possible.

## CREATE YOUR OWN ACTIVITIES

MATERIALS NECESSARY:

EXAMPLES OF ACTIVITIES:

KEY POINTS TO BE EMPHASIZED:

→

# *UNSTRUCTURED PLAY (3-8 YEAR OLDS)*

In unstructured play the child is initiating the activity. You are helping to guide your child toward risk-taking behaviors.

## MOVEMENT ACTIVITIES

MATERIALS:

jungle gym
(monkey bars)

trees

If your child is engaging in these activities, then encourage:
- hanging on the bars as many different ways as possible
- moving to all of the bars as quickly as possible
- climbing as high in the tree as you can; higher than last time
- hanging like clothes on a clothesline.

KEY POINTS:

→ Emphasize the physical challenge of moving on the playthings.

# CLIMBING ACTIVITIES

MATERIALS:

wooden boxes

large rocks

railroad ties

tree trunks

drainage pipes

sturdy packing boxes

playhouse

If your child is engaging in these activities, then encourage:
- moving on the railroad tie as many ways as possible, i.e. hop, skip, jump, walk, etc.
- going inside the pipe at one end and coming out the other 2 times; 3 times; 4 times; etc.
- climbing on the playthings and balancing on one foot; 2 body parts; etc.
- climbing on the playthings and pretending to be a ballerina; a monkey; etc.

KEY POINTS:

→ Stress the fun and challenge of climbing and encourage increasing the level of challenge with each attempt.

# CREATE YOUR OWN ACTIVITIES

MATERIALS NECESSARY:

EXAMPLES OF ACTIVITIES:

KEY POINTS TO BE EMPHASIZED:

# *ORGANIZED PLAY (3-5 YEAR OLDS)*

## WALKING BACKWARD

MATERIALS:

tape line

2 × 4 boards

ACTIVITIES:

Challenge your child with questions such as:
- Can you walk backward in a straight line?
- Can you walk backward around obstacles?
- Can you walk backward like a giant, quiet as a mouse, etc.?

KEY POINTS:

→ Stress how well they dealt with the physical risk of stepping off the line.

# HITTING A BALL OR BALLOON

MATERIALS:

> light weight ball
> or balloon

ACTIVITIES:

Challenge your child with questions such as:
- Can you hit the balloon in the air 5 times? 10 times?
- Can you keep it in the air as you walk around?
- How many times in a row can you keep it in the air?
- Can you touch the ground between each tap of the balloon?
- Can you turn around between each tap?
- What else can you do?

KEY POINTS:

→ Emphasize the fun of trying new things. Point out that missing the balloon is no problem, just try again.

# HOOP ACTIVITIES

MATERIALS:

hula hoop

large tire

ACTIVITIES:

Challenge your child to:
- roll the hoop as far as possible
- roll the hoop and run around it as it rolls
- roll the hoop and run through the hoop as it moves
- roll two hoops at once.

KEY POINTS:

→ Emphasize the fun of the physical challenge of running near or through the hoop. Praise your child for trying new things.

# LUMMI STICKS

MATERIALS:

> lummi sticks
> (8-12 inch rods)

ACTIVITIES:

Provide each child with one lummi stick, and instruct him or her to hold the stick at one end using the thumb and fingers, not the palm. Have child beat the stick to music (adapted from Albemarle, 1979). Challenge the child with questions such as:

- Can you use music of varying speeds?
- Can you beat the stick on the floor? (One pattern would be to have the child hit his or her knee twice, and then hit the floor twice. Continue this pattern.)
- Can you create different patterns?

KEY POINTS:

Stress the fun of setting new patterns and moving at different speeds. Emphasize how important it is to try new activities and enjoy them.

# KANGAROO JUMP

MATERIALS:

```
balance beam

2 × 4 board

rope
```

ACTIVITIES:

Child stands at the side of a beam or a 10-12 ' long line made with floor tape which can be used as a beam substitute. Keep both feet together and jump sideways across the beam. Repeat several times.
- Can you jump with your eyes closed?
- Can you jump backward or forward?
- Can you begin at one end of the beam and jump back and forth to the other end?
- Can you walk on the line as walking a "high wire"?

KEY POINTS:

→ Stress the physical fun and risk of jumping with eyes closed. Encourage new skills even if at first failure may occur (i.e. if the child already knows how to jump forward, have him or her jump backward).

# CREATE YOUR OWN ACTIVITIES

MATERIALS NECESSARY:

EXAMPLES OF ACTIVITIES:

KEY POINTS TO BE EMPHASIZED:

→

# *ORGANIZED PLAY (6-8 YEAR OLDS)*

## CROSSING THE BROOK

MATERIALS:

```
jump ropes
```

ACTIVITIES:

Two lines are made with jump ropes to represent banks of a brook. The brook is narrow at one end and wide at the other. The child begins by jumping over the narrow part and moving on to a wider part as he or she is successful.

- Ask more than one child to jump at a time, competing against each other.
- Place an object on the line representing the bank of the brook. Can the child jump over varying heights as well as varying distances?

KEY POINTS:

→ Stress the fun and challenge of competing against one another as well as the physical risk of missing the rope at a given height.

# RED LIGHT — GREEN LIGHT

MATERIALS:

> none

ACTIVITIES:

Children line up on the starting line. Choose one player to be "It." This player stands on a goal line and counts quickly from one to ten. Upon reaching ten "It" says, "Red Light" and turns to face the class. While "It" counts to ten, the players try to move toward "It", freezing when "Red Light" is heard. If, after calling "Red Light," "It" sees any players moving, those players may be sent back to the starting line. The first player to reach the goal line is the new "It" for the next game.

"It" may not turn around to face the other players before "Red Light" has been called. The counting—"Red Light" sequence must be continued until a player reaches the goal line (adapted from Albemarle, 1979).

- Can you use different forms of movement (i.e. walk, jump, skip, etc.)?

- Can you use a set number of hand claps or allow the leader to play a record and stop it whenever the other players should stop?

- Can you, instead of sending players back to the starting point, have them take a certain number of steps, jumps, skips or whatever to move back toward the starting line?

KEY POINTS:

→ Stress the fun of risking being caught by not returning to the starting point or not stopping when the "Red Light" occurs.

# PRISON DODGEBALL

MATERIALS:

```
bounceable balls
```

ACTIVITIES:

Divide the children into two teams and give each team half the playing area. Each team tries to get their opponent's players out by hitting them with the ball. A player that is hit goes to "prison" which is located behind the opposite team's end line. To get out of "prison" a player must hit a player on the opposite team who then must go to "prison" behind the opposite team. The team that puts all of its opponents in prison first wins (adapted from Albemarle, 1979).

- Require the prisoners to catch a direct pass from their team before they are allowed to throw and hit an opponent.
- Allow players to use the sides as well as the end line as prisons. Do not allow prisoners to move from prison to prison or to move once they have hit the ball.
- If a player throws a ball which is caught by the opposite team, he or she must go to prison.

KEY POINTS:

→ Stress the challenge of succeeding at this task (such as "going to prison") as well as the risk of failing to catch the pass from a teammate. Emphasize how good it feels to work until success is attained.

# SMAUG'S JEWELS

MATERIALS:

```
beanbags
```

ACTIVITIES:

One person chosen as Smaug stands guard over the jewels (beanbags). Everyone else forms a circle and tries to steal the treasure without being tagged. If tagged by Smaug, a player is instantly frozen in place until the end of the game (adapted from Fluegelman, 1976).

- Divide the children into several small groups to play the game. Use several beanbags and two or more Smaugs. Children line up and on a signal run to try to capture the jewels. Once the jewels have been captured, pick a new Smaug. Divide the children into two teams and give each team several beanbags. On a signal, each team tries to steal the other team's jewels. A new game is started after each successful attempt to steal the jewels from the opposite team.

KEY POINTS:

→ Reinforce the importance of trying to capture the jewels. Encourage children to take the risk of trying something new in order to capture the jewels. Stress the fun of physical challenges in group play.

# SHARK

MATERIALS:

```
none
```

ACTIVITIES:

Players line up on a line with one or two players designated as the center players or sharks. The center players yell "Shark" and all the runners try to run to the opposite line, about 15 yards away, without getting tagged. Any player who is tagged joins the center players and becomes a shark. The last player or two left may be used as the sharks for the next game (adapted from Walker, 1980).

- Runners put a scarf or rag in their back pocket or belt. Instead of tagging a runner the shark must pull the "flag." Once the flag is pulled the runner becomes a shark.
- Use set boundaries and if a player runs out of these boundaries he or she is automatically a shark.

KEY POINTS:

→ Stress the risk of being caught and becoming a "shark," and the fun and satisfaction of escape!

# CREATE YOUR OWN ACTIVITIES

MATERIALS NECESSARY:

EXAMPLES OF ACTIVITIES:

KEY POINTS TO BE EMPHASIZED:

→

# 7
# MOTIVATING
# THROUGH PLAY

Key issues to be addressed in this chapter:
- Understanding the Purpose of Play and Games
- Guidelines for Presenting a Problem
- Learning to Change Games
- Modifying Rules and Goals
- Realizing Your Role as a Parent

# UNDERSTANDING THE PURPOSE
# OF PLAY AND GAMES

The purpose of play and games is to provide interaction between your child and the world. Therefore, if you are to help your child use games effectively as a learning medium, then you must understand how to make use of games to enhance achievement motivation. For example, instead of following the tradition of the final goal being winning or losing, you might help your child achieve success by establishing shorter goals at various levels. Intermediate goals such as these are called progressive or sequential goals.

# GUIDELINES FOR PRESENTING A PROBLEM

Challenging children to try new activities can be a great way to motivate them. Challenges are not presented in any particular order. You should take a cue from where your child is and the interests shown. Your judgment is the final factor in deciding which ideas are best suited for the needs and skills of your child. The total number of variations is limited only by your imagination and your child's curiosity. The materials can and should allow the creation of hundreds of different challenges which are appropriate for each and every child.

Some suggestions on how to present a challenge to your child follow:
► Show me how...
► What ways can you...
► How would you...
► See how many different ways you can...
► What can you do with a...
► Make believe you are a...
► Discover different ways you can...
► Can you...
► Who can...
► What does a...
► Show different ways to...
► How else can you...
► See if you can...

# LEARNING TO CHANGE GAMES

Free play and games can both be used to motivate your child to achieve. In order to foster goal-setting behavior, it is important for you to be able to break games down into their component parts. The difficulty of playing games is determined by three components:
► the type of movement necessary,
► the complexity of the rules, and
► the playing strategy.

The simplest activities involve only body movements and use little or no equipment. Watch your child's skill at: running, skipping, jumping, hopping, dodging, twisting, and turning. Most early games use these movements, such as in the preschool grades when dramatic games and tag games are commonly observed. As you encourage your child to participate in these types of activities, be sure to structure the games so that no one is eliminated because of poor performance. The following examples of the game of *"Chase"* will illustrate this point.

The game of *Chase* involves players who are scattered in an open playing area. One player is "It" and chases the other player, trying to tag someone. If "It" tags someone, the person tagged becomes the new "It" and the game continues. At the beginning, you may want to have one *team* be "It," so no one is unsuccessful. As the game progresses, variations may be made to make the game more challenging.

- ► If a player is tagged, that player must hold onto the spot on the body where the touch occurred and chase the other player. This requires greater coordination since only one hand may be used to tag another player.
- ► An area called the *"Zombi Zone"* may be used so that "It" may tag a player either by touching that player's body or forcing that player to run into the *"Zombi Zone."* The difficulty is increased with this variation because the players must avoid both "It" and the *"Zombi Zone."* Additional difficulty can be added with Zombi obstacles such as tires.

As the strategy or complexity of a game changes there may be greater risk-taking. The greater possibility of failure and/or possibility of success is important as children learn about both psychological and physical risks. Caution should be taken not to make the activity so difficult that the chances of failure are greater than success. There should be a 50:50 chance of success in most activities. This 50:50 notion provides the ideal level of hard work and personal effort required to be successful.

Select the level of complexity so that your child is participating within his or her ability or capability. If the game is appropriate, children who expend the effort and use the appropriate skills and strategy will be successful. This hard work should be reinforced, since effort and ability play a part in the child's success.

As the child becomes familiar with *Chase* even other variations can be added. One variation might provide an additional challenge for the child and offer motivation for success. *Touché Turtle* is a variation of the game of *Chase*. The game has been changed to provide more challenge, more motivation to succeed, increasing complexity, and increased activity for the children.

### Touché Turtle

► This game is a more complex version of *Chase,* using the same formation and adding the elements of a "safe" position and "frozen" position.

► A player is "safe" when lying on the back with arms and legs held up in the air and has said, "Dead Turtle." A player is frozen if tagged before getting into the "safe" position.

► A frozen player may be unfrozen by any running player who crawls through the frozen player's legs.

► The "It" role may be switched whenever "It" is tired.

A few examples of possible variations of *Touché Turtle* are given below:

► Change the boundaries to make the playing area larger or smaller.

► Add another tagger so there are two "Its."

► Let the person who is "It" pick a new "It" after tagging three or four players.

► Change the method of moving about the play area (i.e. skip, hop, etc.).

Once your child becomes familiar with the structure of games and the movements necessary in games, more complex games may be tried. Adding equipment is one way to change a game. For example, the same game of *Chase* can be played but now an object is introduced. "It" must now tag the runners by throwing a ball. Once hit, that player becomes the new "It" and must try to tag another player by throwing the ball.

Still more variations can be used with this game to make it even more challenging and difficult. Some suggested variations might be:

► Play the game with a home base or safe spot allowing no more than one person to be on base at a time.

► Introduce a new role so that any player who is hit with the ball becomes "It" and may help the original "It" tag the remaining players. The game would end when all players have been tagged.

► Play with two pieces of cloth hanging from each child's waistband. "It" makes a tag by pulling the cloth strip out of the waistband.

These games introduce the concept of a higher level of playing strategy and the concept of outwitting an opponent. The child must now be concerned with his or her own actions as well as those of an object, and can progress if control of self plus something else occurs.

When the number of rules is increased, more strategy required, or additional players included, the parent must be aware of resetting the goals. When the goals are reset, then the child must be encouraged to take greater risks. This will help your child become more goal-oriented and independent.

With higher goals, your child will know toward what he or she must work. With increased knowledge about the performance the child is increasing his or her motive to achieve. In this instance you must allow your child to take responsibility for his or her actions. Parents do not want their child to blame himself or herself, but want the child to know how to better perform in the future.

# MODIFYING RULES OR GOALS

Rules of games are generally simple and should emphasize actions rather than outcomes. The rules should be relatively simple at first. As your child's skill increases so should the complexity of the rules. Your child may attempt to set his or her own rules. The games may ultimately be made more complex by introducing better defined roles, additional rules, more players, and increased playing strategy.

Games play an important part in developing your child's achievement motivation. They also enhance his or her general motor development. In

selecting games, strive to use games that:
- ► provide for maximum activity by all children who are involved
- ► promote inclusion rather than exclusion
- ► are easily modified

A variety of categories within the game structure may be suggested to help you change games. Regardless of the labels attached to the game categories, there are six areas which have been successfully changed to motivate children:
- ► the number of players
- ► the equipment
- ► the movement pattern (the way players move)
- ► the organizational pattern (the way the game, players, etc. are grouped or organized)
- ► the rules of the game
- ► the purpose of the game

It is possible to provide a wide range of educational experiences by changing the components of one or more of the categories. Your judgment and imagination are the keys to this process.

The following worksheet is provided to help you learn to change various aspects of each child's play. Choose a game, and attempt to change it to meet the developmental level of your children. Then ask your children how they might change the game.

# GAMES WORKSHEET FOR CHILDREN

Ask a child to name a favorite game he or she plays:

Name of game: _____

   Change any one of the following to make the game more challenging. In the early stages ask the child to change only one thing. With practice ask him or her to change more than one thing.

Change from    →    To

Players     _____    _____
Equipment     _____    _____
Way the children move     _____    _____
Way the children are
organized     _____    _____
Purpose of the game     _____    _____
Limitations of the game     _____    _____
Play area (boundaries)     _____    _____

# REALIZING THE ROLE
# OF THE PARENT

Parents should be prepared to help children learn to plan ahead and set goals. In order to be a facilitator, rather than a dictator, you must be able to:
► assess the present capabilities of children
► help children evaluate their own abilities
► help them reset their goals in a realistic fashion.

# KEY CONCEPTS

• Play and games contribute to achievement motivation.
• Help children to use play and games to judge themselves.
• Modify games and play to meet each child's need and growth.

## Suggested Reading

Sheehan, T.J., Alsop, W.L. Educational sport. *Journal of Health Physical Education and Recreation.* May, 1972

Morris, G.S.D. *How to change the games children play.* Minneapolis, Minnesota: Burgess Publishing Company, 1976.

# REFERENCES

Albemarle County Public Schools. *Exploring physical education for elementary children*. Charlottesville, Va.: Albemarle County Public Schools, 1979.

Bryant, Rosalie and Oliver, Eloise McLean. *Complete elementary physical education guide*. New York: Parker Publishing Company, Inc., 1974.

Duval County Public Schools. *Pre-kindergarten, kindergarten, first grade physical education curriculum guide*. Jacksonville, Florida: Authors, 1977-1978.

Fleming, Bonnie Mack, Hamilton, Darlene Softley, and Hicks, JoAnne Deal. *Resources for creative teaching in early childhood education*. New York: Harcourt Brace Jovanovich, Inc., 1977.

Fluegelman, Andrew (Ed.). *The new games book*. New York: Doubleday and Company, Inc., 1976.

Hall, J. Tillman, Sweeny, Nancy Hall, and Esser, Jody Hall. *Until the whistle blows*. Santa Monica, Cal.: Goodyear Publishing Co., Inc., 1976.

Kanawha County Schools. *A guide for the elementary physical education program*. Charleston, W. Va.: Author, 1976.

Kirchner, Glen. *Physical education for elementary school children* (4th ed.). Dubuque, Iowa: William C. Brown Co. Publishers, 1978.

Morris, G.S.D. *How to change the games children play*. Minneapolis, Minn.: Burgess Publishing Co., 1976.

Virginia Beach City Public Schools. *Physical education: first and second grade* (Rev. ed.). Virginia Beach, Virginia: Authors, 1971.

Walker, Pamela. Albemarle County Public Schools. Unpublished manuscript, 1980.

# EPILOGUE

## A Child's Commandments To Parents

1. My hands are small; please don't expect perfection whenever I make a bed, draw a picture, or throw a ball. My legs are short, please slow down so that I can keep up with you.

2. My eyes have not seen the world as yours have. Please let me explore safely; don't restrict me unnecessarily.

3. My feelings are tender; please be sensitive to my needs; don't nag me all day long. You wouldn't want to be nagged for your inquisitiveness.

4. I need your encouragement and praise to grow. Please go easy on the criticism; remember, you can criticize the things I do without criticizing me.

5. Please don't do things over for me. Somehow that makes me feel that my efforts didn't quite measure up to your expectations. I know it's hard, but please don't try to compare me with my brother, or my sister.

—Author Unknown